FORUM FAVORITES

Volume 1

1988

Printed in the United States of America

Foreword

TODAY'S FORUM began with Lois, drafting our first Newsletter on a yellow pad at the old Clearing House. The yellow pad had to rest on her knee because there was only one desk and a table. Never one to complain, she simply went ahead each month, writing all groups to tell them what had been accomplished or proposed.

Lois continued writing the Newsletter for over two years while work increased enormously. A part-time staff member was needed to supplement our wonderful volunteers and we were fortunate enough to get Henrietta from among them. She took over the Newsletter. But as work kept mushrooming, the combined job of Newsletter and the office work was just too much for one person.

Shortly before that I had taken a full-time job in the United Service Organizations' Division of the YWCA National Board and had found it necessary to limit my volunteer work. It had been a wrench to give up my days at the Clearing House, where for almost two years, I had been assigned to corresponding with individuals and groups. More rewarding and stimulating work would have been hard to find. When I went to USO I was unwilling to sever all ties so I clung to my Al-Anon Board of Trustees membership.

One evening in the spring of 1954 after work at USO, I arrived late at a Board meeting. Lois interrupted the discussion to tell me about Henrietta's difficulty and said that the Board had suggested I take over the Newsletter.

Without any hesitation or misgiving I lightheartedly agreed and have always been happy I did. Perhaps if I could have looked ahead and seen the growth of the undertaking I might have paused, at least for a moment. For the first eleven years I worked on it nights and weekends but since I retired from USO, I work at home, giving it practically full time.

The first issue of the Newsletter I edited was that of June, 1954. At the end of 1955, the first full year, 12,210 copies had been mailed in the 12-month period. It is interesting to note that in the single month of December, 1969, the figure almost equalled that of the whole year of 1955, or 11,659 copies. But back in 1954 none of us even dreamed of such growth.

Lois and I worked together that spring to plan a more comprehensive publication than just news of groups and the Clearing House. Somewhere along here the groups were polled and voted to call it the "Al-Anon Family Groups Forum." We decided to have a Step, a Tradition or a Slogan discussion in each issue and Lois suggested I write a monthly "inspirational" article.

That description has always made me a little self-conscious because I so frequently question how anyone who persisted in so many mistakes for so long a time, could inspire anyone. I readily appreciated that such helpful articles would add value, however, and agreed to try. Later it came to me how very right Lois was when she suggested I write such articles. Paul (I Cor. 1:27) said long ago, "God hath chosen the foolish things of the world to confound the wise . . . the weak things to confound the things which are mighty."

All the misdirected efforts to help my husband, the heartaches, the unhappiness and turmoil I had caused and fostered, all that was a costly investment in failure. But it became capital upon which I could draw to prevent others from persevering in similar mistakes. My failures enabled me to explain how our program really should be followed.

And so this book came into being. When Lois proposed to the Board that our 1970 Convention book be a collection of my FORUM articles, her working title was "The Best of Margaret." That name was enthusiastically hailed by many readers. But we since have thought better of attaching any Al-Anon's name to any official publication of our fellowship. That decision was made, not because it would break anonymity, which it would not, but because Al-Anon itself is, and should be, more important than any of its members.

So it is that "Al-Anon's Favorite Forum Editorials" comes to you now. My great love for Al-Anon and my appreciation of all that Al-Anon has meant to me, comes with it. Editing the FORUM all these years has been a privilege impossible to deserve or to describe. Countless numbers of you have added immensely to its helpfulness for without your contributions of letters, experiences and encouragement, the FORUM would never have grown to what it is today.

Thank you and bless you. My love to you all.

Margaret D., Editor

January 7, 1970

Contents

Our Bonus

"LET EVERYONE SWEEP in front of his own door and the whole world will be clean."

That wasn't written about Family Groups and Al-Anons don't aim to clean up the entire world. Most of us came to grief just by trying to take in too much territory.

Either we tried running things with too high a hand, weighed ourselves down unnecessarily by assuming guilt for another's drinking, tried too hard to stop it, or we soothed our deeply hurt feelings with luxurious baths of self-pity. None of it was good.

In our own way, though not as obviously, we were just as excessive as our compulsive drinkers . . . indulgence in hot anger, violent reproach, neurotic frustrations. Our attempt to retreat from the world in order to avoid embarrassment or shame, was exactly as uncontrolled as our partners' drinking.

Whether we acknowledged it or not, ours was a disease too—a mental disorder we'd let ourselves fall into, just as our alcoholics knew they had a deadly disease yet continued to take chances with it.

But through the Twelve Steps, we are learning, or have learned, just to sweep our own doorways. The inventory we now take is our own; we can find enough when we honestly look for it, within ourselves, to keep us busy sweeping only our own dooryards. Over the years we have accumulated enough trash, enough grime and dinginess in an unhealthy aloofness from life, so that we need only concentrate on ourselves. That's our job and it's a big, challenging one.

With the Twelve Steps and the whole Program to use as our broom, we can make our dooryards immaculate. We can bring back sparkle to tired lives, restore hope to beaten creatures who so shortly before thought themselves better dead. We can live again as we were meant to live.

And, sweeping only before our own doors, we can reap the extra reward, share in the bonus of knowing that we are helping to make the whole world clean.

Our Large Place

"I called upon the Lord in distress. The Lord answered me, and set me in a large place." Psalm 118:5.

Like so many of us, did you begin life as a confident, out-going person with a family which meant the world to you and a wide circle of friends, interested in everyone from the grocer to the paper boy?

And, over the years of living with a problem too great for you, did you gradually shut yourself away from your own family, friends, casual acquaintances and any contacts which could be avoided, no matter how flimsy the pretext?

That's what most of us did. We didn't quite realize just how we were narrowing our world until one day realization came that we had built a solid wall between ourselves and our family, our friends and anything and everything outside the tight shells in which we had encased ourselves. Our shells were closer and more confining than those of snapping turtles. Porcupines were soft, companionable pets compared with the bristling creatures we'd become.

For shorter or longer periods, we lived withdrawn. For most of us, the first AA contact pierced the wall but it was only breached, not demolished. The understanding in-stantly felt among other husbands or wives, faced with identical problems, gave us hope. But, as it should be, AA was designed for alcoholics; the help we got was indirect and only partial.

In our Al-Anon Family Groups, however, we find the complete help we so desperately need. The application of the program, while it is still the same program, is designed for us, the sober members of families damaged by alcohol. Here is our opportunity to discuss just how the Steps apply to us, how they are best interpreted for non-alcoholics and we are constantly reminded to practice this program "in all our affairs."

We come to the Family Group in great distress; we learn to call on the Higher Power as we understand that Power, and the immediate hope, release from tension, and the new aim and insight gained from meeting with other members, gives us the knowledge that indeed the Lord has answered us and has set us in a large place.

From the narrow, pressing walls we have built, we see the day when our alcoholics are again their true selves, instead of unhappy slaves to incomprehensible, compulsive drinking. And it isn't too long before we've torn down our walls ourselves, cast off our shells—even though for a few, their alcoholic mates may still persist in drinking.

Truly, we are in a large place, with understanding, hope and faith to keep us in it.

"Kindness in Another's Trouble,
Courage in Our Own."

THE LITTLE-KNOWN Victorian poet, Adam L. Gordon who wrote those lines had about as checkered a career as any of us. Born in the Azores, educated at Oxford, he went to

4

Australia later and joined the Mounted Police. Then he became a member of the House of Assembly.

There's nothing now to show what made him write them. The most skillful amateur steeplechase rider of his day, perhaps a bad spill was responsible.

Most of us have had plenty of ups and downs, and it didn't take a steeplechase to throw us. We did that ourselves with a stupid answer to a tremendous problem. Retreat from life because of fear, self-pity and resentment, is not good for even normal living—how much worse it is, then, for us who live with alcoholics and the consequent distortions of family life.

Our entire Al-Anon Family Group philosophy is indicated, however briefly, in these two lines: kindness, which entails understanding and patience towards others in like circumstances; courage, for ourselves to acknowledge our helplessness, our inability to run our lives alone, much less to direct the lives of wives or husbands; courage to admit our dependence upon a Higher Power to take over the job at which we have failed. And above all, courage to call upon that Higher Power to direct us and to accept direction, however it is given us. We may not like the answer but we ask and obtain the courage to follow it.

In the beginning, when we are freshly stimulated and excited by new hope, release and inspiration, we frequently have a lot of both hope and courage, but before we sink ourselves deeply into the program, we sometimes have

Courage in another's troubles
Kindness in our own.

This marvelous Twelve Step blueprint for a way out of despair provides many directions we glibly accept and quickly pass on to something else without sufficient effort to put those directions to work. Where we fail to live the plan ourselves, where we meet setbacks or defeat, we accord ourselves a less rigid judgment than we give others: we failed because we were tired, because we have to "let go sometimes" and can't always be expected to show absolute control; it has to be our turn occasionally. Thus we excuse ourselves.

It is only by constant, intense study of the whole program that we get the order right again and attain the kindness toward others and the courage in ourselves. When we succeed at this, even though the alcoholic problem with which we live is still an active one, we are given courage to make our lives count; to live in order and decency and not in trembling fear; to hold our heads up, with the sure knowledge that help is at hand when we call upon it; that the Higher Power can, and will, stoop to lift us up, as high as we will let Him.

Knowing Ourselves

THIS MONTH'S STOPPER—"Knowing ourselves helps us to live better with others."—is particularly apt to this issue of the FORUM because it fits so well with the Fourth Step. The fact that it was written for a pamphlet on mental health gives it even more significance as it broadens the application, not just to us, but to anyone struggling with a big problem.

We all know dimly that progress comes only with dissatisfaction: man grew tired of living in a cave so he built himself a house; skins and furs were stiff and clumsy so he wove supple cloth for his attire; the spoken word was too difficult to be his only means of communication so he devised the alphabet and written messages.

6

Back of all these was dissatisfaction, discontent with present circumstances or actual pain. Little as we like to acknowledge it, we must realize that pain is a necessary part of our growth.

Children sometimes grow so quickly they have actual "growing pains," which are lightly dismissed by thoughtless persons. But they are not fun for the one enduring them. Neither is the pain of spiritual growth which also can be attained only through dissatisfaction, unhappiness and a wish to progress.

If we allow ourselves to remain dissatisfied and unhappy, discontented with our lives, to wallow in constant misery and complain endlessly, we waste our opportunity to grow in stature. Life without pain to overcome and spur us on would be static and sterile.

Through suffering, if we accept it as the good it is meant to be, we can grow, can achieve an understanding that success is not just in material things, in living a pleasant, happy life—nice and comfortable as that would be—but in overcoming our own defects of character, in suppressing our selfishness and in living for others rather than for ourselves only.

No one knows better than we the pain of living with an alcoholic problem. But we, who honestly try to practice all Twelve Steps in all our daily affairs, know also that pain is the price we pay for a better and deeper understanding, a richer and more meaningful life.

Real Members

SCARCELY IS THERE a meeting where someone doesn't say, "I used to give a lot of lip-service to the AA program but the Al-Anon Family Group helped me to begin living it."

Many of us recognized the program as a wonderful way of life but since it was labeled "The AA Program" we didn't apply it to ourselves.

Someone once wrote, "One may hold a truth, yet without inwardly possessing it. The formula which we accept will lie sterile in our minds if we do nothing to apply it to the reality which it is intended to serve." This is where we came in.

Most of the program lay sterile in our minds when we used it only to take our partner's inventory; when we admitted only that he was powerless over alcohol but kept feeling we could somehow control or manage his drinking; when we heard AA stories and pointed out their application to our alcoholic partners.

We did more harm than good, although we thought we were helping. We really added to a burden which already was crushing him. We probably even prolonged the excessive drinking, because that was his way of fighting back, just as a child who has been put in the wrong will fight against correction.

But when we applied the Steps and the Program to ourselves, when we finally accepted the fact that we also were powerless over alcohol, and that we needed the Higher Power to help us, that we were given this problem, perhaps, for our own spiritual growth, then and only then did we begin to share in its wonderful workings.

Another person said, "Years ago, we found that loyalty is born of interest and that interest is the child of participation. As long as people work for a cause, and weave something of themselves into the moving fabric, that cause has powerful and lasting friends."

It doesn't much matter if Family Groups have friends, unless those friends are the powerful and lasting kind who have woven something of themselves into their fabric. Family Groups need the kind of friends who work for the cause and it doesn't much matter whether that work is washing up cups after meetings or being willing to speak at other groups, or spending time and thought on newcomers. All jobs have to be done, not just by one or two "old timers" but by each member of the group.

When each of us does his share, all of us benefit from the participation. When all of us participate, each of us gets more out of the program.

Our Children

ARE YOUR CHILDREN being crippled by a parent's alcoholism? It is accepted now as a family disease and since a couple constitutes a family, their marriage suffers from the malady. But the suffering is greater where children complicate the situation.

It is harder to see loved ones suffer than to suffer oneself; it is hard to accept the fact we cannot and should not spare our children all pain. Only by letting them surmount small hurts do we prepare them to surmount greater hurts they cannot avoid. If we try to hide or disguise alcoholism by saying: "Mother has a headache" or "Father isn't well," we fool ourselves. Four words from a neighbor's child, "Your Dad's a drunk," quickly destroy the illusion we tried to create; they make the situation worse by shaking confidence still further.

Parents should learn all they can about the illness and as soon as children are old enough to understand something is abnormal in their homes, should explain as fully as possible what is wrong and what is being done, or can be done.

Parents can and should put away their own fears to

inspire hope in their children. Lois tells of the dark years of Bill's drinking which must have been very difficult for her parents to watch. Yet all through those years Lois's mother constantly told her she believed in Bill and knew he would stop.

Although she died before this happened, her faith in Bill and her certainty of his eventual sobriety was of the greatest comfort to Lois and many times gave her courage to believe herself. That was before the miracle of AA.

If a grown woman can get such comfort and encouragement from inspiration like this, how much more do bewildered and unhappy children need it!

Now that we know what AA can do and has done, we must practice the program closely enough ourselves so that we can help our children by its teachings. The constant use of the Serenity Prayer is a great aid.

Most children are thrilled by the concept of AA and often want to live the program themselves. It is wise to encourage them in this. The Steps, vigilantly and courageously lived, will help us guide our children until the miracle works for us and them.

Help from Going to Meetings

HAVE YOU SOMETIMES thought the Al-Anon program was a bit theoretical, perhaps a mite too idealistic and impractical, and that you had not quite got the help you were seeking?

Some of us thought that in the beginning but fortunately we caught a glimpse of something—we didn't know what, maybe a feeling of warmth and fellowship which made us return again and again.

Then our eyes and ears really began to open. Usually the change came only after a number of meetings, and particularly one where a newcomer sought help. Generally speaking, new male Al-Anons come resentfully and female ones with tears and trembling. But both have the same story: "I've done everything I could to stop the drinking but it gets worse and worse. I can't take it any longer. It's driving me crazy."

When you smiled at the "I did everything I could to stop the drinking," (who knows better than we just what the tremendous understatement "did everything" covers?), perhaps you did not realize just how much the Al-Anon Group had already done for you. Probably the smile was a sort of Mona Lisa one, which stemmed from an honest recognition that such acts were futile trickery, just as we smile at a child pretending he is a grown-up because he's put on his father's hat. But you did smile!

No one can live a normal life without hope; thus if you follow the Al-Anon Family Group suggestion of facing up to your worst fears and looking them right in the eye, you are making progress, for you will see there is a way out. If you think things couldn't be worse, it is likely they'll be better soon because they seldom, if ever, remain the same.

You can free yourself from fear and attain tranquility by rooting out and recognizing just what you fear most. If it is fear that family and friends will learn of a partner's drinking, honest recollection will probably show you that long ago they must surely have recognized that for themselves. If it is fear that he'll lose a job, that fear can be faced and plans made. No matter what the fear is, none is as bad as the nameless ones which keep you churning in turmoil, without direction or hope.

Growth in Family Group philosophy is sometimes slow and unnoticed. It may take an outburst from a bewildered newcomer to show us we have progressed. But the fact that we can smile at our own mistakes proves we have been helped. How much more is available to us if we work at the program, if we study and practice the Steps, say the Serenity Prayer, read and try to understand the pamphlets!

It is very old stuff to say that you get out of something only as much as you put into it. But you'll be surprised at what you'll get if you put yourself into this program: it may be yourself you'll get back. But it will be a more generous, decent, tranquil self and one infinitely more easy for you to live with.

Now Is the Time

IF FAMILY GROUPS have any perfect saints, I have yet to meet one such marvel in my fairly wide experience over a period of years with a number of groups. Most of us quickly realize our goal is perfection. We try to approach it as closely as we can but we do not need to feel we have failed if we cannot quite achieve it.

In trying, we stretch ourselves spiritually. By trying to work all the Steps, the prayer and the slogans of our program, we come closer to what we would like to be than we'd have believed possible a few years ago.

That we sometimes fail is no cause for despair. It has been said, "Of all bad habits, despondency is among the least respectable," so when we do fail we pick ourselves up and immediately begin again. There is no going back to the pre-Group days when we reveled and sank in self-pity and resentment.

We have set ourselves this new goal of serenity and helpfulness to others. Many people feel that Lent is a time of preparation, atonement for past misdeeds and preparation for joy to come. Lent is here, and whatever our creed, now is a good time to concentrate deeply upon our aims.

Why not try working harder at whatever part of the program has been difficult? If it happens that you are diffident, pick out some member of the group and make a real effort at being friendly, or perhaps just listen attentively to a newcomer in trouble.

If your problem is one of acceptance, real work and thought on the Serenity Prayer will help. "Let Go and Let God" will take you a long way toward accepting any situation if you really put God first. Stop trying to run things alone.

Here's an idea: divide up the rest of Lent. After figuring out just where you need the most work on the different parts of the program, concentrate a certain portion of time on each place you wish to improve—a few days on the part where you have begun to improve and a couple of weeks on the toughest spots.

Good and Bad Talks

"I AM JOAN, married to an alcoholic for twenty years. We were happy at first until Ben began drinking. He went from bad to worse until he drank most of the time, practically never was sober. I got afraid to have the children near him. He was in the hospital four times and I began to think of leaving him . . ." Then follows a long, detailed account of perhaps fifteen years of plain and fancy drinking—all too familiar to all of us, winding up with a brief plug for AA and the Family Group in general terms.

How many times have you heard just such a talk, and

how much did it help you or the person making it? Mostly it was simply a tale of woe, better left untold.

Common experience and shared background is the foundation, the true backbone of the help we get from each other. But our talks differ from those of AAs, or should, and too many of us have patterned them after AA speeches.

There they qualify themselves as alcoholics by outlining detailed experience, how sick they were and what they did to get well. We need only say our partners are alcoholic to qualify us. Dwelling on it further wastes time better spent on the program itself, on specific instances of help.

Take me—I could say with truth that I had made myself ill with worry and thought I was losing my mind. That is true. But how much better if I say,

"Strain made me neurotic to the point where I associated changing the sheets on my husband's bed with his starting on a binge. To avoid starting one, I sometimes left them until they were gray and I was sick with shame.

"At the first Family Group meeting I attended, I heard a poised, happy young woman tell how she had done the same thing with her curtains. When she laughed at herself, I suddenly saw I wasn't going insane and went home to change my beds."

Nothing anyone has ever said since has helped me as much as that initial lifting of an intolerable load. And it was lifted because the instance was so specific. In dozens of talks since then, I have found countless others who had similar phobias and were equally hagridden by them. Each time I have told this, one or more of the group has told me of a similar superstition and of a new resolve to overcome it, as I had mine.

Not everyone is as lucky as I was at a first meeting but if you pick out some definite failing, some particular instance of your past and tell it, along with the things which

helped you over the hump, you are bound to reach someone with experience so similar that he will be helped as
dramatically as I was. What satisfaction is equal to that?

We say our program is to help us improve ourselves and
our work is on ourselves. Let us study to see that there is
where we do keep the emphasis, always. Our talks should
be on what we were like, what helped us to change and,
where we had difficulty in the program, how we overcame
those difficulties.

There are few better means of getting the program than
actually making talks at meetings. In order to give help to
others, we must understand and practice the program ourselves. To prepare a really good talk we must sort out and
re-evaluate the whole program and thus it becomes graven
deeper on our minds.

Each of us is capable of either a good or a bad talk. The
person who makes the kind first quoted is exactly as able to
make a helpful one as the person who brings them up out
of their chairs.

It takes only a little more thought, a little more time for
sifting out ideas and selecting particular instances so someone "out there" will be at one with the speaker. Try it,
soon!

What Is Your Favorite Sin?

THE OTHER DAY I came across a little pamphlet headed,
"What Is Your Favorite Sin?" It startled me and I read
on.

"Take your pick: do you think the first and worst is sex?
What about murder, laziness, jealousy, over-indulgence, or
anger, stealing, backbiting?"

I stopped and thought that perhaps my favorite sin was speaking too hastily, being too quick to criticize or comment sharply, but I read on: "These and all the rest have one thing in common. The root of them all is self-centeredness. And Christians believe that Sin in any form is putting yourself ahead of God. So—if your favorite sin is getting you down, don't worry. There is a remedy."

A moment's reflection showed me just how right the pamphlet was—all my failings do come from self-centeredness, although I seldom think of myself as selfish. But I have let worry get me out of balance.

I know now what the trouble is and how to fix it. And I don't believe it was coincidence that the pamphlet came my way while I was thinking especially of the Eleventh Step. I believe the Power Greater than myself was lighting my way.

Choice of Ruts

WHO SAYS ALL RUTS are bad? Somewhere in the North Woods there's a sign which reads "Choose your rut carefully; you'll be in it for the next twenty miles."

I've driven some bad roads, out in the high Rockies, but I've seldom seen one where you could not go at least ten miles an hour. So, even at that worm's pace, a bad rut lasted only two hours.

But what of us, closely tied to alcoholics? We know alcoholism is a permanent disease, which is arrested but never cured. That surely is a thing we cannot change.

It is true we can change the tie, but if we decide to remain with the sufferer—even for only one more week or day—we can change the way we spend that time.

Too many of us have spent years in the old rut of self-pity and resentment. We didn't call it that because those aren't pretty sentiments. It's easier to fool ourselves that we were concerned only about our loved one, more soothing to an already bruised ego.

But with courage and detachment, with the help of the program, we can see what an appalling rut we are, or were, in. Conscious and conscientious practice of all the principles of the program lifts us out of the old, bad rut into a good, healthy way of life in which we have courage to meet whatever comes.

If we choose this new rut we can stay in it, not for twenty but for all the miles that lie ahead, and we can make them happy miles.

What Is Living For?

IN A GRIPPING murder mystery a question, and a statement, jumped off the page at me: "Just what do you think living is for?" and then "The one unforgivable fault is weakness."

I tried to read on but forgot the thriller as realization grew that this question and intimated answer are a ready-made approach to our Family Group Program.

If you think your life is for pleasure, distraction or limited to your own self, then probably you'll never read this article nor be in an Al-Anon Group, because we believe life is for growth, both mental and spiritual.

That growth began, for most of us, when we accepted the fact that compulsive drinking wasn't a weakness but the result of a disease. We grew a little more when we looked within ourselves and found weakness there—weakness in the way we had refused to meet our problem, in the way we had attributed all fault to the alcoholic and in prolonged self-pity.

The Steps for us have been steps up to a higher plane. From them we have learned we are less than perfect ourselves and likely to remain so but that, following the Steps, we can gain courage and serenity to make our lives count toward good and not add to the evil already in the world.

We can become helpers, not helped; givers, not takers. Gradually we leave weakness behind us and learn that growth, although painful, is worth the suffering.

Just what do *you* think living is for?

Our Slips Are Showing

WHEN I TOOK a half-slip from a drawer my husband asked what it was. "They used to be petticoats but now they're half-slips," I answered.

"Half-slips are something AAs can't have," he said and I quickly agreed. And the quip stuck in my mind: I decided that while AAs can't have half-slips, Family Groupers can— and sometimes do.

If we have spent even a short time only in conscientiously following our program, trying to live the Steps to the fullest, we are not likely to fall back completely into the old, bad ways.

But every time we worry about next month, or say a quick and cutting thing to someone or let personal prejudice distort our thinking, we are indulging in a half-slip.

And half-slips turn into real slips if we persist in them.

Christmas Stocking

EVERYONE LOVES TO WATCH a child pull treasures from his Christmas stocking. The rubber ball, bubble pipe, space-gun or tiny doll are ordinary enough toys but to the child, each is a separate surprise and enchantment.

If our Family Group contribution could be wrapped in tangible form and put in our Christmas stockings, I wonder if we'd be happy to view a year's work in a field where such marvelous opportunities are given to each of us.

Would we open up package after package of friends and strangers made happier by the time, effort and thought given to them by us at moments when they desperately needed comfort and hope? Would we find unexpected little what-nots, tucked in here and there, which represented thoughtful comments at meetings? Would we find a shining star which meant we had met every challenge—or even just most of them?

I know the temptation of letting some one else take on the new person at meetings and no one knows better that it's hard to contribute when you're tired: no idea seems worth putting into words. But perhaps that's your unique opportunity to reach someone else by telling of the very thing which disheartened you.

"To whom much is given, much is expected" may sound like old stuff but it's old because it's good. We have been given much in this program of ours and I hope all of you find much to enchant you in this make-believe Christmas stocking. May you all find pride in the hope, help and joy you have given others.

Why I Believe in Family Groups

AT THE St. Louis Convention last July, someone asked me why, when her husband was successfully sober in AA for six years, she needed a Family Group?

I thought a moment and said AA was then celebrating its 20th Birthday and after all those years of Bill's sobriety, Lois still found help in Al-Anon Family Group work and in living our program. Undoubtedly there was a better answer but I couldn't think of one at the time.

Right now I can't speak of any such period of sustained sobriety. But knowing myself, I believe if there were years of it behind us, I still would need to keep close contact with this work. Without the numerous eye-openers every meeting affords, without the constant jabs which come from realizing another's courage when my own is failing, without the many sidelights on how to meet and overcome difficulties which each talk gives, I'm sure I would, sooner or later, slip back into my old complacency. And what is more disgusting than complacency?

This program, properly lived, first helps us meet the problem of living with alcoholism. It doesn't stop there or it isn't being lived properly. It is a program of spiritual growth, one which helps us meet every other problem life brings. It has already helped me with the first problem and with others not connected with alcoholism.

When the day comes that I can say there's been a year, or six or ten, of sobriety in our home, I'll be saying it at a Family Group meeting, because there's where I keep finding the way to living as I like to live.

God's Help

A GREAT PART of our Family Group program, like its parent AA, is spiritual. Some people have difficulty in accepting that spirituality. They approach it as a reluctant swimmer risks one toe in a cold sea.

For the most part, I plunged wholeheartedly into the spiritual thinking. What bothered me was the practical side, the recognition that I was powerless over alcohol.

One troublesome thought, however, kept popping up to distract me from complete spiritual serenity: when things were bad, I'd comfort myself by remembering God's promise that He never would give me a burden too heavy for me to bear. And I'd say a prayer and feel better.

But sometimes the thought would stray across my mind, "What of those people who commit suicide, or go insane? Their burdens *must* have been too heavy for them." Then I'd pray some more and the nagging doubt would go, although a shadow of it remained to trouble me.

Since this is my own particular corner of the FORUM, and I've never pretended to be wise, I can admit here that it wasn't too long ago that, suddenly, the answer to this question flashed into my mind. Now it seems incredible that I ever was bothered about it or that I should have been so long in finding the answer.

It's such a simple one: the burden will never be too great *if* you ask God's help in bearing it and if you *earn* that help by following His Will.

God's Will

HAVE YOU EVER been troubled, wondering just what is God's will?

We say in the Third Step that we "turn our will and our lives over to the care of God as we understand Him," which means that we'll try to live according to His will. More specifically, in the Eleventh Step we "pray only for knowledge of His will for us and the power to carry that out."

But what is God's will?

He seldom speaks directly to us, although He has done so in the past. We still live in this world, and there are decisions which must be made. We can't sit back passively and wait for a flaming sword to direct our paths.

A lot of the time decisions aren't very important. Whether we walk to a given place or take the car can't matter much to God. But where issues and futures and serious things are at stake, how can we be sure we are following God's will and not just our own in a subconscious way?

That used to bother me, as it did my husband. But we have found the answer—a sure way to make certain it is God's will and not ours. Like so many other important things, it's a very simple way:

All that's necessary for us is to do *everything* we do *in* God's name and *for* God. Then we can't go wrong.

To the Newcomer

TO MANY OF US, the most difficult thing about a partner's drinking was the persistent thought, "If he really loved me, he wouldn't drink that way."

At first we didn't know a compulsive disease was responsible but even when we learned alcoholism is now accepted as the fourth largest health problem, the nagging sense of being rejected still was present.

Steinbeck says, in *East of Eden,* "I think everyone in the world to a large or small extent, has felt rejection. And with rejection comes anger, and with anger some kind of crime in revenge for the rejection, and with the crime guilt—and there is the story of mankind. I think that if rejection could be amputated, the human would not be what he is . . . one child, refused the love he craves, kicks the cat and hides his secret guilt; and another steals so that money will make him loved; and a third conquers the world—and always the guilt and revenge and more guilt."

I don't suppose many of us went around kicking cats or stealing but most of us in our own devious ways, did things in frustrated anger we were ashamed of. If *he* didn't love us enough to be sober, *we'd* show him it didn't matter. Rejection, pure and simple: a childish game of tit for tat. But we're now too old for such games.

Al-Anon Family Groups sooner or later teach us that alcoholic drinking is not a deliberate reflection of indifference, that it has nothing to do with love. When we reach this haven of comprehension, we are freed of the sense of rejection, of guilt and of anger we have fostered so long.

We have time and spirit, once we stop fighting ourselves, to develop an understanding, a sympathy and a serenity that makes our homes pleasanter places for all.

The Night I Felt Like God

COLLEGE SOPHOMORES are noted for thinking they know everything and apparently I was no exception because, as one, I caught a glimpse of what God frequently must feel when He considers mankind and its mistakes. It seems appropriate this month, when we are reflecting on the Eleventh Step, to recall that feeling and the help it has brought me all these long years.

I was in charge of costumes for the Annual Follies, a job much too big for me and one never before given a sophomore. I worked incredibly hard, especially on costumes for eight fireflies. We even used chiffon instead of paper cambric, so you can see it was the high point of the production.

Delicate, fairy-like, red-haired girls were chosen for the dance. I stayed with them until I saw they were all ready for their entrance. Then I went up to a vantage point, high in the wings, where I could look down and gloat.

Poor things—the flooring between their dressing room and the stage was cold and splintery to bare feet, so they slipped into flapping galoshes for the run to the stage.

Seven lovely sprites, all orange and flame, leaped to center stage and danced about a flickering fire. The eighth clunked along, complete with galoshes!

Into my head, without a pause, jumped the thought: "This must be the way God feels when we do something wrong. *He's* done everything but, given free will, *we* mess up all His work."

Many times since that night, fortunately before I've leaped, complete with galoshes, I've remembered that sorrowful moment for something lovely marred by thoughtlessness. And I've kept myself from messing up His plans for me.

I haven't always been successful but at least I caught a glimpse of what being really close to Him could mean and I've tried to get closer still.

Family Group Needed

A RECENT LETTER, signed but with no address, gave me great distress and concern. It was extremely vehement and I wish space permitted giving it in full. She wrote:

"Of all the tommyrot ever started, it's that people (the so-called alcoholics) are sick. They are no more sick than one who indulges in any other vice or is a glutton of any kind. A customer, a woman who goes on binges, came into my place and said:

" 'I am sick; I need treatment. I'm an alcoholic.' I said, 'There's no such thing. God did not make anyone a slave to any vice—you want to drink.' 'Yes,' she answered, 'it helps me to forget.'

". . . telling people they are sick only gives them an excuse to drink. To break any habit takes only determination and prayer. They're sick? My eye!"

Eventually ignorance such as this, I know, will be eradicated: with AA, the Al-Anon groups and the National Committee on Alcoholism all working to educate the world on this problem, it won't be many years before such a point of view is as outdated as the idea that the world is flat.

After all, it isn't too many years since mental illness was considered a disgrace, hidden because of shame, and mentally ill persons many times were treated less well than animals. Education in the field of alcoholism will surely accomplish as much for alcoholics.

But what concerned and bothered me most was the antagonism displayed—the ill-will shown. It worries me because I feel the author needs Family Group help. She sounds sick and hurt and fearful herself, and there's no way to reach her at present.

Since she was interested enough to write Al-Anon, perhaps she would be interested enough to go to an Al-Anon meeting in her home town sometime and we'll have a chance to help her.

Loving Kindness

SCRIPTURE TELLS US that even "a cup of cold water, given in My Name," will be rewarded. In Family Groups we are more likely to offer a cup of hot coffee with simple human kindness but the spirit is exactly the same, because whatever we offer is given through love and understanding. Our reward usually is immediate.

When we have attained serenity through practicing the Twelve Steps, it is so apparent to the disheartened newcomer or to the older member going through a difficult period, that each is reassured. Each knows he, too, can reach the same goal by embracing the program or by digging in deeper to recapture it.

Our own lives still may be troubled with the same old problem but we have learned, or are learning, to live peacefully with it. We may have other new and serious difficulties but we are learning to accept them with fortitude and the sure knowledge that they can be surmounted.

Gaining serenity is hard; holding fast to it frequently is difficult, too, but, in the main, we're grasping some of it.

Those troubled spirits who come to us in their despair

can sense our serenity. When they learn that our story, our life experience, duplicates their own, they get a strong ray of hope that their lives can and will be brighter, their burden lighter.

To help them look up with hopefulness, to show them they can gain that same serenity, to know they no longer live in despair—that is our immediate reward. And what a reward for just a simple, human kindness!

Easy Does It

IN YOUNGER and sillier days, my sister and I once charged up a Colorado mountain at the same fast pace we walked Chicago's flat streets. We did for a few hundred feet, that is. We then stopped, gasping for breath until our hearts stopped pounding like pile-drivers. We resumed at a sensible rate and made our goal.

Sometimes people try to swallow the Al-Anon Family Group program as heedlessly as we ignored altitude. A sort of mental indigestion is the usual result because this program is solid meat—not a quick lunch designed for four rapid gulps.

Most of us are too upset and too wrapped up in personal worries when we come into the group to be ready immediately for the Twelve Steps. Those take time and thought and plenty of reflection on what our true aim and goals are. Acceptance of them comes when we relax and lean on a Higher Power, not when we frantically tread a squirrel cage of activity.

Beginning in childhood, with fairy tales and legends, like the Hare and the Tortoise, Bruce and the Spider, and a dozen others, we constantly are cautioned to go slowly and steadily, to accept defeat and make another valiant try. That holds good for Family Group work—Easy Does It, but *do* it, and *keep on doing it.*

Bits of the program sometimes come easily and at once. Other times we seem to have it all in our grasp and following it is simple. We are lifted up and float through the days.

Then, perhaps because we have slackened our efforts, a day comes when we fall into old habits again and we feel we have failed. That is the day to take stock, to see where we went wrong and how we can put things right.

By now, too many persons have been lifted from despair by this program for any of us to have any serious doubt of its effectiveness. What we need is to follow it closely and steadily: it will work for all of us if we let it.

Live and Let Live

IN OUR MEETINGS we hear and speak a lot about tolerance. The dictionary definition of it is, "the disposition to be patient and fair toward those whose opinions or practices differ from one's own."

That's a good beginning, to my way of thinking, but it's just the first step toward true tolerance. Certainly if we close our minds to everything with which we do not agree, if we deny others the right to think differently, if we never examine our beliefs to see if, perhaps, we can widen our horizons, we ought to be cabbages, planted in neat rows in a truck garden, rather than valued members of such groups as Al-Anon. Cabbages have their place but also they have their limitations.

What we seek in Al-Anon is continuous growth, mental

and spiritual. We cannot achieve this growth unless we seek to enlarge our comprehension, not only of our principles but of people. And we cannot attain this comprehension without a concentrated effort toward understanding.

The French have a saying that to understand all is to forgive all. While differing from ourselves is not in itself a matter for forgiveness, once we understand another person thoroughly, we are more in sympathy with him. We accept the differences between us—frequently we grow in stature by this acceptance.

Learning to accept less-than-perfection in other people is, however, sometimes child's play when compared with accepting it in ourselves. Yet if we are to Live and Let Live, it seems to me that we should number ourselves among those who should be accepted. Many of us can readily understand failure in others but still make ourselves miserable over our own failures. Frustration and pressure build up in us because we fall short of our aim and cannot understand why.

Instead of aiming at instant perfection, if we were to choose one failing and work toward overcoming it, we would eventually succeed. We then could attack the next. Even if each effort took a year, it wouldn't be too long before most faults were much improved.

So, let's remember that tolerance is understanding—of ourselves as well as of others.

Christmas Wish

FROM THE TIME when the Three Wise Men, bearing gifts, first followed the star to Bethlehem, Christmas has been a time of giving. We would find it difficult today, to make gifts of gold, frankincense or myrrh, and indeed, after the ravages of years, any gift at all sometimes seems beyond our power to manage.

But we do have gifts, those given us and those to give others, no matter how bankrupt we seem—the gift of gratitude that we have been led to Al-Anon, and the God-given opportunity we have there to help others; the gift of hope we have attained, which has strengthened us to attend another's dire need; the gift of serenity which has helped us and steadied our families as well.

But above these, the greatest gift of all is within each one's power, and that is the great gift of prayer. We've been led to believe again, or more strongly than ever before, in the Higher Power. We can pray that every person still in need of the precious gifts we have been given, will be guided our way and given them, too.

My Christmas wish is that I, and all of you, will always be grateful for these gifts, and above all, will be fervent in our prayers for others. God bless Al-Anon and all its members—a true Christmas to all of us.

Values

EVEN FOR SO SIMPLE a visit as an overnight stay, we plan our luggage and what we'll pack. How, then, shall we plan, with a bright New Year ahead? It will come only a day at a time but there's a year of days in which to accomplish our aim.

"What is life but a choice of values? We never lose anything by leaving it behind—we take it along in another form." Those are good words to remember in mapping out a new year.

Al-Anon has changed many forms for many of us.

Through it, we have learned that the shame we formerly suffered has changed to sympathy for another's illness. We have learned that anger and frustration can change to understanding and tranquility. We have learned that what we thought a curse has led us to our deepest happiness. Nothing has changed but our own selves, when we worked toward changing ourselves.

Once we recognize that our time, energies and capabilities are limited, we increase our chances for satisfaction by choosing to work on something within our scope.

For instance, I always wanted a lovely singing voice—that, to me, was the ultimate gift. As a child I sang constantly but gradually learned (from others; I sounded fine to me) that even with two baskets and a boy to help, I could never carry a tune.

I was unhappy over this until it came to me that if I worked hard enough at it, I might learn to make words sing for me and perhaps, through them, help another. No work would have changed my inability to sing but work *has* helped me to write.

Thus, in the year ahead, we can take along with us, in the best form possible, all that we have experienced this far. If we are still resentful, we can seek out something to replace that resentment, something which will help us and others too; if we are discouraged, we can aim at a year of hope and faith.

By concentrating on love and understanding, we can forget ourselves and lose ourselves in this most wonderful program.

Let's choose our values for 1957 carefully, and a Happy New Year to all in doing it.

The Enemy Within

WE ALL KNOW the parable of the householder who sowed his fields and whose servant came to him saying, "Master, did you not sow good seed? How then are there weeds in thy fields?" and the reply was, "An enemy hath done this thing."

We are like that man: we began with good seed—hope, faith and confidence that we could keep our lives strong and straight, but then the enemy came and we succumbed to doubt, fear and despair.

What we did not realize was that the enemy was within us, our human failure to cope with our own problems. Our excuse and explanation was a ready one: if we had not had to struggle with alcoholism, we'd have remained strong and sure.

In Al-Anon we have learned it is possible to live with this problem and return to our first surety of hope and faith. We have seen this happen to hundreds around us; once we accept the fact that our problems are separate from those of the alcoholic, a Higher Power leads us to the solution of our own.

As alcoholism is a progressive disease, so is that of our own neuroses: as long as we allow ourselves to wallow in self-pity and despair, as long as we distractedly run about trying to manage another's life, just that long are we letting the enemy within us stifle our power to climb into a haven of hope and serenity.

Once we truly admit we have *let ourselves* slip into despair because of something out of our control, we gain the first victory over that enemy. When we rely upon the Higher Power for help to rise from the pit we have dug ouselves, we get that help in abundance.

In Al-Anon we can see that others have obtained the strength they need and are living lives of faith and peace. When we gain this serenity for ourselves, it spreads to others—to our children and our families, and even to the alcoholic who needs it so terribly.

Recognition of the enemy within ourselves is our first step. After that the Higher Power will help us to go forward to live with restored hope, faith and tranquility.

Seeds of Today

"ALL THE FLOWERS of all the tomorrows are in the seeds of today." I ran across that recently when I was feeling about as hopeless as it's possible to feel.

Without realizing it, I had allowed myself to slip back into negative thinking where I looked forward only to more of what was making me unhappy. Suddenly I realized that if I continued as I was, those tomorrows *would* be grim and black—but they needn't be: Al-Anon had taught me different ways.

Al-Anon seeds, planted over the years, sprouted right then, anew.

First to pop up was the fact that I was not facing years of anxiety but only the one, present moment and it was gone while I thought of it—nothing had happened in it, either, except for good.

I made myself look back at other times and realized I'd managed to live through them, so likely I'd live through this. I sorted out my worst fears and looked them straight in the eye—individually, they didn't seem as bad as the mountain of evil I'd made them into.

Had I continued my merry-go-round of worry, I'd have

been ill—my present days would still have been full of the weeds of despair and heartbreak. But Al-Anon teaching pulled me up by my bootstraps so that today hope and courage are at my command.

Time, Strength and Opportunity

> "Grant me strength, time and opportunity always to correct what I have acquired, always to extend its domain; for knowledge is immense and the spirit of man can extend infinitely to enrich itself daily with new requirements. Today he can discover his errors of yesterday and tomorrow he may obtain a new light on what he thinks himself sure of today."

Much as these lines sound as if quoted from a talk to Al-Anon members, they really are taken from the oath and prayer of a Jewish physician, over eight hundred years ago.

More than most people, we who have lived with an alcoholic problem, have acquired habits and traits which need correction. Time was when we knew no better but even a short while in Al-Anon has shown us that most of the things we formerly did were actually as harmful to ourselves as to the alcoholic.

So, strength, time and opportunity to correct these failures are needed by each of us.

As we learn, through our program, to accept alcoholism as a disease and the alcoholic as a sick person, we learn also how to condition our own response to the situation. Anger, fear, resentment and self-pity were doubly harmful weapons against it; most times they made that bad situation virtually impossible.

But as we have enriched ourselves through knowledge

and understanding, we have extended our horizons so that we can better recognize and cope with our problems. We require more of ourselves than an immediate, self-indulgent response to disagreeable circumstances.

By the new light we quickly attain in Al-Anon, we can correct our errors of yesterday. By diligent application of our Steps and Traditions, we can gain further light, because ours is a program of endless growth, with limitless possibilities.

Doing God's Work

READING ALBERT C. CLIFFE's "Let Go and Let God" (not, so far as I know, connected with AA), I came upon these lines concerning the power of prayer:

> *"Don't expect an angel suddenly to appear in person, but know and believe with all your heart that God works through ordinary folk like you and me, and that it is through ordinary people that good will come to you."*

Suddenly it came to me how right and how natural it is that help should come to us that way. Indeed, how else could we expect it to come? Since we are all children of God, He is in all of us, whether or not we are conscious of it.

I always prayed for help with the drinking problem in our home. But I prayed specifically for a miracle: a flaming sword suddenly thrust between my husband and a drink, scaring him green, so that he'd never touch another drop—something like that would have satisfied me completely.

Sometimes such spectacular visions do happen; they didn't in our case, but a quite ordinary miracle did and I got the help I needed so urgently. It came from the very people around me—exactly the ones I had long been trying to avoid, through shame and ignorance.

Through my fellow Al-Anon members I learned that alcoholism definitely is a disease, not a character defect. I learned that but for the Grace of God, I too, might have been a victim of alcoholism—with more difficult problems and a stiffer personal fight for control than that of the wife of a sufferer.

I learned that any one could contract this disease, just as unaccountably as one could be afflicted with heart trouble, arthritis or cancer.

With the realization that my husband had acquired this vicious disease, as he might have any of a dozen others, entirely independently of me, I soon stopped burdening myself with a feeling of guilt or self-pity for having chosen an alcoholic, with all the resultant problems and heartaches.

We have no supermen or superwomen in my group—we are a very commonplace gathering of ordinary persons, a fair cross-section of life today. But these ordinary people brought me my miracle. Living the Al-Anon program and following the Steps, we are cultivating God in ourselves and thus we are privileged to do His Work.

Picture of a Resentment

Is THERE EVEN one person alive who does not meet with an occasional upset? It may be of minor or major importance—a pinprick or a real blow but it is how we react to such upsets that we shape our lives: if the milk doesn't come in time for breakfast, do we snap at the children, are we short with our partners and generally dim the brightness of a new day? Or do we quickly realize that it is relatively unimportant and we can plan a substitute?

Generally speaking, it isn't what happens that counts, but what we do about it. If we allow things to affect us unduly, if we harp on what bothers us, we are fostering a resentment—we are allowing a pinprick to become a stab at our hearts.

People are not always careful to say exactly what they mean, so misunderstandings are bound to occur and wrong impressions are frequently given. Recently such a situation was created between two friends: one spoke quickly, the other was hurt and communication between them stopped. Immediately everything was magnified—each thought the other wrong; the first thought the second was being unreasonably difficult and the second that she was being taken advantage of. But each brooded over the other's attitude. That was a few weeks ago but by now everything the other does is examined in the light of a possible slight.

Instead of determining the original fault, as we do in Al-Anon, and accepting the responsibility for our share in it and making amends, each is carrying a grudge and fostering a resentment which is spoiling a friendship.

"Each day is a fresh beginning—each day is the world made new." If we teach ourselves to live actively with this approach to our daily intercourse with others, we'll really be practicing the Al-Anon program. We'll have no time nor wish to burden ourselves with yesterday's problems.

Are You in Your Second Childhood?

A FRIEND OF MINE once lamented that "it was practically impossible to keep a baby in the house. Before you realize it, they have become children."

Children also, grow up too fast, without knowing the wonderful things they leave behind them: their marvelous, built-in sense of justice for one thing, for who ever heard of children resenting punishment they knew they'd earned? Most lose their complete faith in their parents' power to guard them, for another, and their acceptance of all the world as a friend for a third.

We had these qualities once ourselves but somewhere along the dusty way we left them behind and took to resentments, hurt pride and a rat-race of worrying.

We have been told that we have only to ask for help and we shall receive it—that unless we become as little children we shall not enter the Kingdom of Heaven. What more do we need be told?

We know we have a Higher Power, ready to help us, just waiting to be called on. We cannot go back to our first childhood as we have shed too many skins since then, but there is a second childhood for all of us, which is a rebirth of faith and hope and trust. Let's hurry toward it.

Growing in Stature

"ALL TRULY WISE thoughts have been thought already thousands of times; but to make them really ours, we must think them over again honestly, till they take firm root in our personal experience."

I wish I had written that but Goethe did it first. There is nothing really new in our Program. It was taken whole-cloth from AA. AA got it in bits and pieces from the Sermon on the Mount, from the Oxford Movement and a dozen other sources. It was only new as AA and new as Al-Anon.

In our despair and heartbreak, it came to us as a life-and-sanity-saving, brand-new philosophy and we swallowed it whole, in great, stimulating gulps. What we understood, we put to work immediately and the wonder is that so much of it succeeded so quickly—most of us can easily think of dozens of newcomers who were completely changed by only a meeting or two.

But as we spent months and years following our Program, we absorbed more and more of it until we reached a deeper understanding; its teachings took "firm root in our personal experience."

This deeper understanding gave more and stronger support to us. Al-Anon's teachings enabled us to help others in the same state in which we once lived.

We didn't need anything new—we simply needed to make this truly great Program really ours by thinking and living it honestly.

Whose Story Do You Tell?

SOME TWO and a half thousand years ago, Joel exhorted his people "to rend your heart and not your garments." On a recent trip I was thinking of him as I listened to a couple of so-called "Al-Anon stories" at a meeting.

Two women spoke for a half hour each and it seems incredible that in that time neither mentioned what Al-Anon had done to help her.

Obviously the program had been successful with each, as both were fluent and poised—but each confined herself to her husband's drinking career and how nervous she had become.

To me it was unbelievable that they spent so much time rending their garments over what, happily for each, was over and done with, instead of searching their hearts for what had brought about a happy state.

Neither told anything new about a drinking career—after all, *is* there anything new to be said about one? Neither picked out one particular piece of the program and said, "This is how it worked for me and this is how I went about attacking my problem."

All of us have been in identical circumstances and it would help if we were told exactly how someone else benefited from applying the program.

Joel later promised that God "will restore to you the years that the locust hath eaten." Certainly no one will question that promise when he sees what miracles of tranquility the practice of this program brings to Al-Anon members.

But to those who still are entertaining the locusts, it is difficult to see how the miracle comes about. It would help tremendously if our members singled out the vital points of inspiration, the motivating ideas which aided them in their time of trial and made their talks about them.

Good Talks

As we told you last month, Al-Anon talks can be, and too often are, merely a repetition of past or present sorrows. It may be that such a talk helps the person giving it, though that is questionable, but certainly it is not the ideal speech.

Sketching the background is important and has its place, but it is merely the foundation of the whole talk.

The best talk, the one which helps most people to the highest degree, is the one which brings out just how the program works and how the speaker follows it.

Like Gaul, a good speech may be divided into three parts: "How sick I was. How well I am. What helped me to get well." Of those three parts the emphasis should be on what helped me get well: the Serenity Prayer, the First Step, the Inventory or whatever it was.

For some, a slogan did it and others found their help in the group spirit. But whatever started one of us to regain command of ourselves may well be the very thing to lead another into quiet waters.

The thing which impresses everyone new to Al-Anon is the utter honesty and simplicity of our members—it is never polished phrases which win adherents. We have no need of facile speakers; it may even be that too smooth a speech loses force, so that none of us need fear to talk when asked to do so.

All any of us needs is to spend enough time in analyzing how the program works; then words to tell of the miracle will come.

If one single phrase of a talk sheds light for another person that talk is a good one, though the speaker is halting in delivery. Ease in speaking comes with experience so we all improve with time.

Carrying the message to others, sharing our experiences, is the most important part of our 12th Step work and all we need to help us is some thoughtful time in preparing our talks.

Living the Program

NOTHING WAS EVER TRUER than that oldie, "You can't give what you haven't got." And it is particularly true of our Al-Anon program. If you do not live it yourself, you cannot show another person how to do so; tinkling cymbals and sounding brass are a full symphonic orchestra when compared with the chant of an Al-Anon member who gives only lip service to the program. Gaps and false notes inevitably come through.

If we say we are powerless over alcohol, and are turning our lives and will over to the care of God as we understand Him, and yet try to manage everything; if we ask God to remove our shortcomings and do nothing toward this end ourselves; if we hurt others and wholly ignore making amends; if we simply talk about the program during meetings and then forget it the rest of the time—nothing can cover up the emptiness of our words.

In the Army they say you can fool a General and all the other top brass but you can't fool the GIs. It is the same with us: we might fool someone who knows nothing about living with an alcoholic; we might appear saintly martyrs to outsiders but to those in great need of real help, unless we have grasped the truths we talk about, and applied them to our daily living, we are whistling in the wind.

An old Chinese proverb says, "If I hear it, I forget it; if I see it, I remember. If I do it, I know it." Only by living the program, day in and day out, can we really know it and only when we know the program can we give help to others.

When we have really "Let Go and Let God," have truly accepted "Thy Will, not mine," there is a quiet conviction which comes through even to those in the depths and they are lifted up. If we live this program, we can give it to others.

A Full Meal

IN JAPANESE prisoner-of-war camps, perhaps by necessity, rations finally shrank to a couple of ounces of rice a day. Our unhappy, starving prisoners pulled in their belts and dreamed of a full meal.

When liberation came, almost their first thought was, "Now we can have a full meal." So they might have, because the liberators brought plenty with them, but doctors said no—solid food in any quantity would make them sicker than they were and they must be physically conditioned to cope with a full meal.

Those people come to mind when I read or hear complaints about unanswered prayers. One way or another, many of us foul ourselves up with worldly cares until our spiritual tolerance is equivalent to a couple of ounces of rice.

Whether this sag comes because we are tried beyond our strength or because we lose perspective, is unimportant. Our prayers mostly are concerned with material things— better jobs, more money, a better place to live; the time for them is always NOW: we feel we deserve them and have a right to ask for them.

But think for a moment what would happen if all these prayers were granted simultaneously. Our Al-Anon program is one of spiritual growth and we know the Higher Power can restore us to sanity, but how ready would we be, were we suddenly deluged with material gifts?

It seems to me we cannot hope for overnight success— such growth in our blessings necessarily is slow; we must earn it. We must condition our spirits for it.

To me, the Higher Power is a great linguist, capable of translating every prayer into terms that are best for us: our cries for immediate, material help are answered, perhaps, with the gift of a little more patience with our lot in life; we are permitted to see that things of the spirit have more value than those of the body; we are given a true perspective.

I believe all the things we hope for will come to us when we are ready for them, when they will be for our real good—not now when they might enmesh us in more trouble.

If we accept the Higher Power as having greater wisdom than ours, and if we are willing to place His Will above our own, we then must wait until we are spiritually conditioned for our "full meal."

Faith and Hope

"Faith is the substance of things hoped for, the evidence of things not seen."

Although these words were written nearly two thousand years ago, men had lived by faith and hope long before the words ever were set down on parchment. Men are living by them now in these days of uneasy peace. And come what may, men will continue to live by them as long as they walk the earth.

Men must have faith and hope to endure life's hazards. Men have existed on minimum amounts of food and water, really too scant to sustain life, but as long as their spirits were strong, they hung on to a spark of life until relief came.

No one was mean enough to discourage the survivors of Bataan—no one could heartlessly disturb a child's faith that his mother can help him in all his troubles. Why, then, do we mortally wound ourselves by dimming our faith and hope for a better life?

We would not snatch hope from another's frantic grasp. We would not kill faith in any one eagerly seeking help. But we murder both in our own selves when we allow doubts of the alcoholic to muddy our thinking.

Al-Anon teaches us, and has proved many times over, that sobriety can be won by those who desire it enough; it has charted ways to help us through the dusty roads which lead eventually to our goal of happy, united homes; it offers a guide to serenity and self-mastery, which are priceless aids to daily living.

All this is ours if we throw ourselves wholeheartedly into our program. We can begin with only a spark of hope, a glimmer of faith—and through honest study and practice of Al-Anon thinking, we can foster that spark and that glimmer into a blaze of hope and faith which lights our lives and those about us.

What Really Counts

HAVE YOU EVER refrained from doing something you wanted to do or thought you should do, because you were "just one person and it wouldn't count"?

Even with hundreds of millions of persons on this earth, each one of us is separate and distinct from every other—one soon learns to differentiate even between identical twins.

And, with all the evidence that Creation was planned, not accidental happenstance, it seems to me that there's a reason for this wide diversity among individuals.

We believe a Power Greater Than Ourselves runs the universe, so it is easy to believe that, as each of us was made different, each of us was given different capabilities. I believe that each was given a job to do and the ability to do it, if we draw upon the Higher Power.

It may be that one line of one FORUM will deeply affect and help one person, and I shall have accomplished my job. It may be that one of your talks, at one meeting, will change the life of someone in the group, and your work will have been done.

I don't know what my job in life is, nor yours, but I do know we each have one. I know that only we can do our own job. Since we don't know when that opportunity comes, let's not pass up the chance to do it, by thinking, "I'm just one person who doesn't count." Rather let's think, "This is a job worth doing—I might be the only person in the world to do this specific thing."

Knowing Ourselves

IT FREQUENTLY has seemed to me that Villon was bragging when he wrote "I know all things, save myself." But, complex and individualistic as he was, for all I know he may have written it in a true spirit of deep humility: meant he knew all things save the most important one.

Certainly knowing ourselves is most important to us. Many of us first came to Al-Anon to find the non-existent secret of how to stop our mates' drinking. We thought there was a magic button we could learn to press and their lives and ours would be changed.

The lives of those of us in Al-Anon *were* changed but not by a magic button. We found we were powerless over alcohol and alcoholics, too, but learned to know ourselves and have kept on improving the acquaintance.

When we recognized the worry over a drinking partner as really an acute concern for our own security and well-being, when we saw that we ourselves were causing as much of our mental and physical turmoil as the alcoholic was doing, we were not proud, and soon learned we'd change ourselves only by studying and practicing the Twelve Steps.

Knowing ourselves shows that we didn't need to make scenes, nag or scold: that energy put into such nonsense was better used to strive for tranquility; serenity could be achieved if we worked at it.

We had come to think of ourselves as good managers and the only one in the family with sound judgment.

But Al-Anon showed us that, for all our good management, our lives still were unmanageable. It took the help of the Higher Power, and the humility to ask for that help, before our lives began to straighten out.

We discovered that frequently we had been Managing Mammas because we liked to be—now we see it often is more fun to sit beside the driver than to drive.

Not all that we learned about ourselves was bad. And, most important of all, we learned that we could learn. With every week of working the Al-Anon program we obtain deeper insight into ourselves and our families.

With new serenity and acceptance of others for what they are, we become more content and many of these new qualities brush off on our mates and help them to help themselves to lasting sobriety.

From Me to Me, with Love

GIVE YOURSELF the best Christmas present in the world—even if you are broke, you can afford it, though it is a priceless gift. In fact you can't afford not to give it to yourself.

This best of all possible gifts is a tranquil mind. You can't go out and buy it. You have to earn it for yourself with daily mental discipline and rigid self-control. Al-Anon has guideposts for you in the Serenity and in the St. Francis of Assisi prayers.

None of us would be in Al-Anon if our lives had run in smooth waters. We have real problems, I agree, but don't turn them into anxieties by churning them over and over. That way lies madness—many of us feared that's the way we were going, until Al-Anon. Fortunately we found that fellowship, and hope.

When we put honest thought and study into the program, we began to sort out the things we couldn't change; when we really worked the program we sought to accept those things; not to rebel against them. What we could change, we did.

But this is a continuing process. Basic problems have a way of changing from year to year so that we need to keep accepting—it's not an over-and-done-with job when we overcome one. We need to keep distinguishing those things we can change from those we can't. We can't always do this alone but we have a Higher Power waiting to lend a hand, just for the asking.

Whether or not you cause your own turmoil, only you can give yourself a tranquil mind and an accepting heart. Begin now, today, and by Christmas you'll be well on your way to that most priceless gift.

Our Program Has Everything

SOMETIMES OUR PROGRAM seems to me like the case of the preacher whose son was asked how his father could originate a different sermon every Sunday, and the boy lightly replied, "He doesn't—it's the same old one—he just hollers in different places."

Undoubtedly it is the same old program we follow: nothing has been changed in the Steps since they were adopted, and the slogans have been around a long time, too. But the good part about all of it is, that when a lift is needed, the program furnishes it.

When we are feeling frantically helpless, we are reminded that the Higher Power can help us; when we are feeling smug, the Inventory Step jumps up and flags our attention; when we are in a dizzy maze of futile wonderings, the Serenity Prayer calms us and reminds us to sort out the things we can change from those we can't and to ask for wisdom to know the difference. First Things First and Easy Does It are vital warnings when we tend to take in too much territory and are like children grabbing for everything in sight.

Whatever happens to us, some part of the program applies. All we need to do is quietly reflect a bit and the help we need will jump to our attention and "holler" in the right place.

An Invaluable Education

"THE BUSINESS of education is making people uncomfortable." At first glance such a statement sounds wholly ridiculous and unreasonable; but apply it to our program and it begins to make sense: before Al-Anon most of us quite smugly felt ourselves no less than perfect; any personal shortcoming quickly was dismissed with the self-pitying thought: "It's not my fault—it's because Joe drinks."

Too many sound people, in countless talks, have admitted feeling just that way, for us not to confess freely there were plenty of things wrong with us.

It took the education of Al-Anon to make us uncomfortable enough to sort out cause and effect and to realize the cause was not always someone else's drinking. It was a cause buried within us, perhaps from childhood, which had gradually emerged and grown until it could be recognized.

When people get uncomfortable enough about anything, the sensible person does something about it. So with Al-Anons and their self-pity, their nagging and their devious, behind-the-scenes efforts to manage partners.

Al-Anon teaches a hands-off policy—except on the body to which the hands are attached. Al-Anon teaches that self-pity is self-destructive beyond words, and any meeting furnishes proof enough that someone else is in worse case than we.

Al-Anon teaches that nagging is bad for the nagger but is hopeless for the nagee, so it's time worse than wasted.

If Al-Anon education makes us thoroughly uncomfortable, uncomfortable enough so that we begin to study the program, then it truly is an invaluable education.

Failure Has Its Place

THE IDEA THAT HE, or she, is less than perfect, seldom dawns on the neophyte. But even within the span of a few weeks, enough of the Al-Anon program penetrates one's thinking so thoroughly that we get caught with our imperfections showing.

Essentially perfection is what we are striving for. We

must try to put ourselves in perfect accord with our God and our fellow man.

Progress toward that goal is measured by the amount of thought and action we put into the program. If we confine Al-Anon thinking and practice to meeting nights, progress can be made—because the program is one of growth—but it will be slow.

However, if we channel our efforts toward absorbing as much of the program as we are able to do, day by day, we'll get there faster.

No one, even after years of practice, ever lives our philosophy completely, all of the time. Human error thrusts itself in, and we sometimes become irritated or angry. If we were living the program in its entirety, we'd have enough vision to overcome these interruptions to our serenity.

But however far we fall short of our goal, if we have grasped even a minor part of the program we still have made progress. Each small success in practicing it makes the next one easier.

The thing we need to be conscious of is that we all fail sometimes. It's not how badly we fail nor how wantonly, that counts. To recognize that through failing we learn where we should be alert for danger is the important thing. If we accept these failures as challenges to further growth, then they will serve as steps to success.

Comparison Shopping

HAVE YOU EVER made a comparison-inventory of your own progress and accomplishments, through Al-Anon, and your partner's progress and accomplishments, through AA?

Each of us in Al-Anon realizes that we are not the only one singled out to bear almost intolerable burdens. We realize, too, that the alcoholic also has his own frightful burden and his own private war.

We start even, more or less, from there. But beyond that, the two problems are completely different—poles apart, in fact.

The alcoholic is suffering from one of the world's most insidious diseases and is fighting a twenty-four hour daily battle against a compulsion almost beyond his strength.

We are free of the physical aspects of the disease but none the less are fighting twenty-four hours daily against real, tough, heartbreaking situations.

The big difference is that we have the advantage of being able to fight with a more or less normal outlook: at least it is not complicated by a driving urge to do something against our will.

Sure, sober alcoholics still are difficult to live with. But ask yourself which of us, even without the alcoholic's specific ailment and handicaps, is a constant dream of delight?

So, the next time your mate irritates you thoroughly, pause, consider, do a little comparison-shopping. Ask yourself if you are making as much, or more progress, as he or she is, in the daily battle to win victory, to earn a big share of the new way of life.

Strength

"IN QUIETNESS and in confidence shall be thy strength." What better goal could we have than quiet, confident strength? Think about the older members of your group, who have really studied our Al-Anon program and made it part of their daily lives, and you will have proof that this goal can be attained.

You weren't around when they first came to meetings, so you can't tell whether they were the kind who talked incessantly, monopolizing meetings, or the walled-in kind who said nothing. Each variety presents its own difficulties but perhaps it's a little easier to help someone when you know what's bothering him.

But whether his complaints flowed incessantly like a mountain torrent or, like me, were silently shrieked inside a tightly-shut clamshell, each of us came to Al-Anon for help.

We were an unattractive mess of self-pity, out of touch and out of kilter with ordinary life. We were the only one whose laundryman didn't come; the only one whose child caught cold; the only one married to a sot—everything had equal power to upset us.

It was only when we could stand ourselves no longer that we really exposed ourselves to Al-Anon. We, too, "hit bottom" and the only way out was up.

We relaxed a little, our minds opened a fraction to what we were told and gradually a healthy, hopeful outlook was regained. We stopped complaining, either verbally or silently. Some part of the program, the First Step, Serenity Prayer or a slogan made sense and we began with that and went on to other parts.

Before too long, maybe months and maybe a year or so, we found ourselves possessed of an inner quietness and confidence which we could depend on to be strong enough to see us through anything. If you have not yet reached this goal for yourself, be very sure that it nevertheless is there to be reached: quiet confidence in yourself, your mate, in life and in the Higher Power will be your strength and it will carry you through.

Time to Think

RECENTLY I HAD a most inconvenient, painful and frightening experience: all I did was take a single step on bad curbing and I ended up with my best foot forward in a fifteen-pound cast.

The next eleven days I spent in the hospital, thinking it over. That accident couldn't have happened at a worse time: it came square in the middle of a week's meetings which had been planned for nearly a year.

Ten minutes before it happened, I'd have said that nothing on earth could have prevented my attendance but I missed all of it and lived through it.

No one who knows me would ever confuse me with a Pollyanna, but just eleven days, with plenty of time to think, gave me some new outlooks on life.

For one thing, I developed flu but since bedrest is indicated for that, and I was in bed anyhow, I got over it much more quickly and completely than I'd have done at home. I was right there, handy, when it was time for penicillin shots. There were nurse's aides to see that I drank plenty of juices and took my pills. So I recovered in record time. One bonus for the accident.

The second was the time to think, of which I spoke. When I got over my initial self-pity, I had time to think how fortunate I was that, landing as I did, I hadn't broken both wrists as well as my foot and have been completely helpless. I had time to thank God that no car had been coming along or I'd have been run over. I had time to thank Him I'd got off so easily.

And I went on to think that such things may not necessarily be accidental—perhaps I needed such a thing to jolt my thinking . . . as perhaps I'd also needed the jolts of living with an alcoholic to throw me out of an accustomed rut into the searchings and disciplines of Al-Anon.

I decided that things happen for the best if we ourselves do not waste our opportunities, if we search for the good in every experience and put it to use.

Had I lived a tranquil, normal life, I'd probably be unbearably smug; had I not found Al-Anon, I'd likely have become a shrew and at best would have matured only partially.

It came to me that, just as my accident was not wholly waste, neither was the unhappiness I had endured, if I myself did not allow it to be.

There's Always a Last One

IT IS DIFFICULT to imagine a shock greater than one receives if a partner has had some success on the AA program and then suffers a slip. To the normal person, free of the awful compulsion to drink, the AA program is so logical and foolproof that ignoring it seems wantonly extravagant and wilful. It is impossible to understand why anyone would trifle with such a plan.

Fortunately, he doesn't have to understand. But he does have to accept, and our Al-Anon program and emphasis on the Steps help in this acceptance. And even while the slip is taking place, the Al-Anon member is in much better case than ever before: he has a fellow-member to whom to turn for help and in whom to confide if he is driven to confiding.

There are meetings to attend, where one can obtain help and guidance. There are the Al-Anon books to read and the many helpful booklets.

And since AA helps nearly nine out of every ten members, there is the great percentage that one's partner will be one of the fortunates. These fortunates all stop drinking some time, and one can always hope that this slip will be the last one.

What We're Here For

IT SEEMS CERTAIN to me that we were put into this world to grow in two directions: first physically and second, but most important, spiritually. Otherwise our Creator would have planned differently and, if my mythology is sound, we'd perhaps spring, like Minerva, from the forehead of Jove. As it is we grow from helpless, speechless infants; it takes months and years to learn to walk easily from here to there or to make ourselves quickly understood. It's a long process to adulthood.

We are not creatures of accident. We were created by that Higher Power, whom I call God, and He surely put us here to grow. God doesn't *find* good in us accidentally—rather He puts good in us and gives us the privilege of fostering and increasing it. Whenever we let life get us down—so that we do mean or careless things to others—we defeat our primary purpose in life; we shrink rather than grow.

When we live Al-Anon sincerely and fully, practice the Twelve Steps as perfectly as we are able, we grow up spiritually, too, and fulfill the purpose for which we are here.

A Sourdough's Self Discipline

YEARS AGO, before Al-Anon or even AA, a friend of mine set his private plane down in the back-country of Alaska. There he met up with an old "sourdough" who taught him a lesson he never forgot—one which has stayed with me for many, many years—and incidentally is one of the backbone maxims of our fellowship.

During Bob's two-day visit with the old bachelor in his primitive cabin hundreds of miles from nowhere, he learned that his host received his mail—regularly, all in one huge batch—on one day, each year! The mail consisted mostly of his hometown daily newspapers.

Bob said, "When all those papers arrive, I bet you have a field day, poring through them to catch up on what's been happening."

"Oh no," the old fellow replied, "Quite the contrary. That way it would be all over in a few days. No, sir! I just make myself take it easy . . . I live my life one day at a time. First, I sort them according to date, with the oldest papers first. Then each morning at breakfast, for the whole year, I have a fresh newspaper and they last until the next delivery."

He never slipped—even when there was a murder or an investigation of something hot. He never peeked ahead at the next day's edition to see what was going to "happen." It was all news to him and he made it last.

Somehow he's never really been out of my mind in the years since Bob told me about him. I have always admired his self-discipline in waiting and making his papers last.

I know we need the same sort of self-discipline as that old sourdough in his back-country cabin. I believe we need to live each day as it comes, determined that just for that day we won't let our Al-Anon principles slip from mind but make sure to practice them perfectly. If we do this every day, one day at a time, we will make the program last the year 'round for us too!

All Human Beings Make Mistakes

A LITTLE BOY answered the doorbell one day, invited the visitor into the house, hunted up his mother and said there was someone in the living room. When asked who it was, he replied, "I don't know, but I believe it is a human being."

If we were all more ready to accept ourselves and each other as human beings, there'd be more happiness and less tension in our lives. Certainly we should aim at perfection—should not take failures with complacence. We should evaluate them to discover the cause, but not be crushed by them.

Have you ever stopped to think that a lot of trouble can be caused for yourself, or for others, by expecting too much? Either way leads to heartaches and headaches.

If you rely on a notoriously careless friend to do an exacting job, you'll feel let down if nothing much is accomplished. If you plan to do a dozen things in one day but only finish ten, you are left with a sense of failure.

But perhaps you should have chosen a different person for the exacting task and should have scheduled fewer things for yourself.

Groups, too, get into difficulties because some members expect perfection in all the others: they say, "After all, we are striving for spiritual growth and if those members 'have got the program,' why do they act that way?"

I believe it's quite possible that those people do "have the program" but just slipped momentarily and it shouldn't be held against them.

If we had the program better ourselves we mightn't be annoyed at others. They are human beings.

Browning said, "A man's reach should exceed his grasp, or what's a heaven for?" So, if we constantly, and quite properly, reach for perfection, we shouldn't castigate ourselves and others for constantly falling short.

If we remember that only God makes no mistakes, we can accept ourselves, and our fellowmen, as human beings, with much more happiness and contentment all around.

Counting Our Blessings

WHY ARE WE so often afraid of seeming to be sentimental or complacent if we congratulate ourselves for what we have gained from our Al-Anon philosophy? Are we afraid of being thought Pollyannas, or "corny?" Or do we think we have no reason for congratulations?

Many Al-Anon members are married to still-active alcoholics; many have spent a dozen or more years with a drinking problem which has just lately been resolved.

Scars are deep but the wounds are not mortal hurts. Perhaps if they were examined in a true light, they would prove to mark opportunities for spiritual growth, and so are like a soldier's battle ribbons. Growth seldom is accomplished without pain.

Once in a while, it seems to me, we'd do well to meditate for a moment and simply count our blessings—forget the failings—and dwell on what we have that is good.

No matter how bad the drinking problem is, we are at least alive to cope with it. And just being alive is our first blessing.

A Blast of Fresh Air

A SEXTON had difficulty heating the church and when the minister complimented him on the comfortable warmth he finally achieved, the sexton said, "I shoveled and shoveled and couldn't get the heat to 50. Then I opened all the doors and windows and it got frigid. But when I had thoroughly aired the church and shut it up again, the temperature went right up to 70."

If you've been stewing around in an uncomfortable bog of "bills, bills, bills" or "kids, kids, kids" or even "drunks, drunks, drunks," why not try the sexton's trick? Stop everything and let a blast of fresh air into your mind. You aren't getting anywhere, anyhow, just by worrying.

Blank your mind of whatever it is that is nagging at you. Then take a new, quiet look at it, ask the Higher Power for help and you'll find your answer.

If We Choose

STEPHEN VINCENT BENET once wrote, "Our earth is but a small star in the great universe. Yet of it we can make, if we choose, a planet unvexed by war, untroubled by hunger or fear, undivided by senseless distinctions . . ." I believe he was dead right but that it will take some doing to make such a world.

I believe each one of us is but an infinitesimal part of the billions who inhabit our "small star in the great universe," but we are an important part and, if we choose, we can make our lives count toward ending war, hunger, fear and the divisions of senseless distinctions among us.

I believe, if we choose, we can conquer fear and to me, that is the place to begin. I believe this also takes some doing. It was fear which made us the wrecks we were when we came to Al-Anon—fear of the past, present and future, of public and private opinion, of ourselves and of our mates and of the world at large.

By following the program as it gradually unfolds, by practicing the Steps more honestly and whole-heartedly, we gradually overcome these fears. Like all human beings, we have failures because we sometimes falter in these observances and fear returns.

We do know, however, that fear can be vanquished by constant effort. We know that life without fear is a heavenly blessing and the whole world is a different place when we have peace of mind. We can have these things, if we choose.

Learning from Experience

"EXPERIENCE IS THE best teacher" has been around too long not to have a lot of truth in it. It would have been forgotten long since if it didn't make sense.

"Experience is the best teacher," certainly—but whose experience, is the question. Having the same old ones, for twenty years, maybe—"Joe's drunk again"—obviously didn't teach many of us how to cope with it, how to live with it, for a long time.

What we need, when we come to Al-Anon, is to gain experience in a big, big way—and fast.

We can learn more ways to handle our situation from a dozen group meetings, than we previously did in a decade. Going it alone is a long hard road because it involves making the same old mistakes.

What we need is to learn how experienced Al-Anoners have handled situations similar to ours, how they have handled themselves successfully.

Definitely, we can learn by experience. But that experience need not be our own.

A "Do It Yourself" Method for Al-Anon

"MANY PEOPLE are unhappy in marriage because they expected to get too much with too little effort," counseled David R. Mace, in discussing rocky marriages.

Just change "marriage" to "Al-Anon," and this could have been written about some members and some groups.

We have all seen a number of people attend a few meetings; sit back passively and neither participate in discussions nor try to follow the program.

Then they stay away because they were disappointed. They expected to get too much, for too little effort. In fact, they had expected to find the magic key to a mate's sobriety, in answer to the simple question, "How do you make some one stop drinking?"

We know there's no answer to that question. But we do know that through Al-Anon, we can find peace for ourselves—even though the drinking continues, and furthermore, that frequently our own peace impinges upon the alcoholic and he seeks peace for himself, through AA.

Groups, too, sometimes expect too much for too little effort. Keeping a group active and healthy takes serious work by each and every member; they have to contribute ideas, leadership and time.

No group can grow and broaden its influence if everything is left to one or two, or even five or six, members. Actually, it takes considerable time for a group to develop to its fullest usefulness. But even if one remains small, for months or indeed for years, who is to say that that group is not aiding its members?

Many groups always will be small for one reason or another, but nevertheless they still can exert great influence.

Let's really apply a "Do It Yourself" Al-Anon method for ourselves and also for our groups, so that we'll never expect too much, for too little effort.

First Things First

ONE OF THE very first things that struck us, in Al-Anon, with terrific force, was that we were not all alone in the turmoiled world of alcoholism. We had thought that we alone had been singled out to cope with a bewildering problem.

We even thought that wilfulness, lack of self-control, or just plain cussedness, was responsible for excessive drinking and we were ashamed and confused. In our sick despair, most of us had crawled into a hole and tried to pull as much of it in after us as was possible. But at Al-Anon we found scores of others, each with the selfsame problem. That gave us our first, immediate lift.

Then came the revelation that alcoholism definitely is a disease! We learned further that while this disease positively cannot be cured, still it can be arrested and that gave us hope.

For some of us that hope was dampened from time to time, when a partner, having sought and found AA help, returned to uncontrolled drinking. Still others had hope dimmed when a partner refused to recognize that there was a problem and continued to drink excessively.

But the knowledge that a disease was responsible helped us to see the whole problem in a different perspective.

One thing we can never learn in Al-Anon is to understand the tremendous compulsion to continue drinking that an alcholic has, once one drop of alcohol is imbibed. Only another alcoholic can understand that.

Also we can never learn, at Al-Anon or anywhere else for that matter, how to stop an alcoholic's drinking. That definitely is his problem and only he can solve it.

With the help of others similarly situated, and with the hope we get from knowing that approximately 300,000 problem drinkers have found a new life in AA, we learn to stop our frantic efforts to force sobriety upon our mates.

We learn to turn our energies upon ourselves, and to accept what we cannot change in others. First Things First means, for us, that our first responsibility is to ourselves and it is upon ourselves that each of us works in Al-Anon.

Quality of Prayer

MANY TIMES at our own, as well as at AA meetings, I have heard people talk of "gimme prayers" as if they were worthless. Speaking only for myself, I believe they could not be more wrong because I cannot think God considers any prayer worthless.

Just as most children creep before they walk, and walk

before they run, so we progress spiritually from "gimme" prayers to selfless ones where we ask only to know God's Will and to follow it. No one says the child is wasting his time creeping—he's learning, just as we have to learn to pray.

Further, I cannot see that it is wrong to ask for material help, when the Lord's Prayer itself contains our plea for daily bread. I believe we get beyond the point of asking for purely material things just as some of our members are able to thank God for their having married an alcoholic and thus learning about our program. In all honesty, I'd have been glad to be spared that: some day I may attain this peak but I do thank Him for what acceptance I have managed to develop.

Prayer, to me, is a learning process. If we put our hearts and minds into praying properly, I am sure we progress in the spiritual quality of prayer. Some prayers are more deeply meaningful than others, and thus more valuable, but I am convinced that any prayer at all is better than none.

Make Straight the Way

A LONG TIME AGO a voice in the wilderness cried, "Prepare ye the way of the Lord, make His paths straight. Every valley shall be filled, and every mountain and hill shall be brought low; and the crooked shall be made straight and the rough ways shall be made smooth."

We may have heard these words frequently, without realizing that in ancient times, much of this actually was done when a king visited. All the people leveled paths through hills and mountains, filled valleys, smoothed roads.

This straightening the way was done a hundred years ago when American railroads pushed rights-of-way across the country. And even today we repeat the process with gigantic roadbuilding projects.

We are not engineers and only use the roads—so what has this to do with Al-Anon? Well, we all have our personal mountains and valleys within us and rough roads to be made smooth. We came into Al-Anon for many reasons but remained for the serenity we found.

We have accumulated mountains of resentments. Some are well overgrown with the green of envy of others more fortunately placed. We have valleys of despair into which we sometimes fall. No road is smooth when strewn with self-pity and ill will.

Al-Anon is the road to "the Higher Power which we call God." Let us then make straight the way: no bulldozer can level the mountain of resentment but straight thinking can push it away.

Fill the Valley of Despair with hope, and rise above immediate limitations. Say the Serenity Prayer and change rebellion to acceptance.

Remember that "This, too, shall pass," and forget to dwell on how horrible this life is.

Few things smooth roads, or brighten lives as much as helping others: if we forget self and remember to do things for others, we'll soon be on our own smooth road.

So, let's make straight the way. All we need is the will to do it—for Al-Anon has given us the blueprint.

Al-Anon Has Answers

WHAT DO YOU DO when you're sizzling angry? If someone has offended you, do you blast back at that person? Do you freeze up into an outraged icicle? Or do you concentrate on "paying him back?"

Over the years I've either tried or seen all these methods used and never much admired any. I'd always got away as fast as possible when angered and then pitched into a job I usually put off because I hate it, like cleaning out the refrigerator or degreasing the oven . . . anything I could put my back into. For me, this worked fairly well but now I've progressed.

Al-Anon has mental aids to calmness and control: the Serenity Prayer comes first. Even though I begin saying it with lip service only, I keep repeating it like "a rose is a rose is a rose." Somewhere along the line, one of the ideas catches up, either the idea of God and then my "mad" seems petty, or I wonder if what happened is a thing I can or can't change and I go on to the courage part.

The slogans are a handy tool too: Easy Does It is always applicable. I can't tell myself to take it easy if I'm yelling. First Things First is good too. I stop to think what really caused the fracas; I may have contributed to it and if I recognize I helped start the fire, I can't be eager to add more fuel.

Somewhere in Al-Anon's teachings there's an answer. It may not be an easy one. But any answer is better than keeping on at a full rolling boil.

Squares and Grannys—In and Out of Al-Anon

Do YOU EVER tie a square knot, but pull and find it's a granny? That's what I usually do; only on the third or fourth try, do I get my square knot. If I didn't know better, I'd swear I do exactly the same thing each time—they just turn out differently.

Whenever my square knot turns out a granny, precisely

the same thought pops into my mind: this is why people have trouble with the program; this is why they question if Al-Anon always works.

They think they're giving it the same attention as always, following suggestions as carefully as usual and giving the program first place in their thoughts. But I don't believe they are.

When Al-Anons get discouraged this way, I believe they've allowed other things to creep in to distract them, so that they've taken a wrong turn, just as I've done with my string.

Maybe they've left Al-Anon at the door of the meeting room and are not using it in their daily lives.

When Al-Anon thinking dominates our daily lives, when God is left to run His world, which He created, in the way He wants it run, then we have no need to question the results. Everything falls into its proper place; there are no wrong turnings and our square knots are always square.

Who Can "Carry the Message?"

TO CARRY the message of Al-Anon to others is one of the greatest privileges and most rewarding experiences of our entire program. But remember, "You can't give what you haven't got." In order to communicate the message successfully, there are three basics:

First, that you know and accept and can prove that our message is authentic, intelligent and effective. Since all Al-Anon teaching emphasizes that we are in this program to grow spiritually ourselves, your message will be distorted if you are still seeking only a way to sobriety for your mate. That is not authentic Al-Anon, although it's what brought most members into the fellowship originally.

The effectiveness of Al-Anon's program is demonstrated in any meeting of a serious group which is really working at it: just contrast the serenity of even a three-months member with the confused turmoil of a newcomer.

As for the intelligence of the program, no stupidity or blind spots could persist in it with so many people giving it the real workout they do; the strength and growth of our movement proves its sense.

Second basic is that you study and actually live the program in every way. You may know that alcoholism is a disease, but if you continue to act resentfully and to permit self-pity in yourself, your message of hope to another will be meaningless.

Third basic is that you carry the message to others in language they understand. Successful communication is a two-way deal; unless one gives and another receives, the message is lost. If your belief in Al-Anon is strong and clear, you don't need eloquence to put it in deathless prose—the meaning will get across.

Al-Anon philosophy is simple. It is a program for spiritual growth; we work it for the benefit we obtain from it, and joyfully accept any side-benefits it brings. Of ourselves, we are frequently helpless but we have a Higher Power upon whom we can always rely.

So, equipped with this sure knowledge and the inspiration of the Higher Power, YOU can carry the message.

Who's a Failure?

IF YOU'VE NEVER been discouraged, never felt that really living the Al-Anon program is beyond you, then these ideas are not for you. They are for those persons who, tried beyond their strength, slip a bit in control and revert to pre–Al-Anon behavior.

A very large number of our members are married to active alcoholics; they have come to Al-Anon, have found help in it and a measure of serenity. For the most part, they are able to manage themselves well, keep fairly quiet when the alcoholic activity is most active. But occasionally something gives—and they let go.

Does this mean they "haven't got the program?" It may, but I don't believe it has to mean that. I believe it means they are human beings. I'm always sorry when I hear or read of an Al-Anoner becoming discouraged because he's blown his top under considerable provocation.

I think the thing to do under these circumstances is to get one's self in hand as quickly as possible, go back to Al-Anon and AA first principles, and stop feeling we are worthless and our Al-Anon work has been in vain.

To me, the Higher Power means God, and I believe He made the world and the men in it. I believe He also made angels. But I'm sure He made the two different: when He created angels, He made them pure spirits, but to man He gave human nature and free will. Since I'm certain He knew what He was doing, I'm also certain He does not expect the same things of each.

Angels were made perfect at the beginning but to man is given the chance to approach perfection. If man takes two steps forward and slips half a step back, I do not believe God brands him a failure; I believe He gives him courage to try again, to do a little better than before.

If I'm even only half right (and, as always, these chats here are purely my personal opinions) I think it a great pity to allow discouragement to overwhelm one and to accept the burden of defeat.

It makes sense to me that if God had wanted man to be

perfect with no effort of his own, He'd have created him
that way.

As long as we keep trying for perfection, even though we
miss it occasionally, or even frequently, if the effort is
honest and sincere, I don't think God considers us failures.

Failure is in giving up, in not trying—the rest, I believe,
is just the human nature God gave us which is our opportunity for spiritual growth.

The Glory of Al-Anon

THERE ARE MANY wonderful things about Al-Anon but to
me, one of the most remarkable, and yet the most charac-
teristic, is the feeling that "You are a stranger here but
once."

To most of us, twenty minutes after we have walked into
an Al-Anon meeting, be it in Orleans, Massachusetts, or
Missoula, Montana, there is a sense of being completely at
home and of being at ease with people exactly like ourselves.

We may not immediately grasp why these crazy people
laugh at tragedy, such as our pitiful tale of a mate who
hides bottles, breaks promises and spends rent money on a
binge. But, somehow, we sense there is understanding in
that laughter and it is not long before we can eke out a
smile ourselves.

We may not find ourselves in complete accord with
every person in the group, but that is not necessary. If
there is just a single person there to whom we spark, that is
sufficient—that person can shed light in our dark places
and lift us over the humps.

Should you find yourself completely out of sympathy

with an entire group, and if you live where there are others, why not try another and perhaps find you like it better?

But if there is no other group available, either start a new one or try digging in your heels and find something you like about the one you are in. Go to at least six meetings before you decide the group is not for you.

The glory of Al-Anon is that there's something in it for everyone; while you are learning about the program, the others are learning, too, and perhaps you'll find you misjudged some of them at first.

Steps to Heaven

I AM ABOUT as musical as a cow but music has always interested me. Odd bits and pieces of it stick in my mind and I love stories about it.

Take Debussy and his "Gradus au Parnassum," from the Children's Corner: I wouldn't have known, myself, that the whole thing is made up of fingering exercises and scales, to improve technique. He just put them together in such a way that a real, musical composition resulted whereby children could be trapped into the best kind of practice, all the time thinking they were "playing a piece."

Maybe the smart ones who knew Latin figured out that the title "Steps to Heaven" boiled down to "practice makes perfect" but they improved, too, as they played.

And that's where I am grateful to Debussy and his sly imagery. For years I have thought of our 12 Steps as Steps to Heaven. We must practice them diligently unless we are to revert to our previous discord.

In this constant practice we strengthen our technique for harmonious, sane living. Given enough time and effort on working the Steps and a healthy, confident self-command will result just as surely as running scales will help a pianist.

We are not children. We do not have to be trapped into practicing this program. Just remembering the hell we made for ourselves of life before it, is enough to keep it in the forefront of our minds. But thinking of it as our Steps to Heaven is a very happy thought to me.

No Little Plans

"MAKE NO little plans. They have no magic to stir men's blood and, probably, of themselves, will not be realized. Aim high in hope and work, remembering that a noble diagram once recorded will never die, but long after we are gone, will be a living thing."

Daniel Hudson Burnham was an architect so he did not have me in mind when he wrote that but it's been one of my three "words to live by."

"The way to spiritual growth is to do two impossible things a day" and "A man's reach should exceed his grasp or what's a Heaven for?" are the other two. All three have the same idea and the same spur: a man needs to stretch himself, to be bigger than he naturally is; he may not be comfortable in the stretching but if he settles just for comfort, he may as well have remained an infant who yells when he's damp or hungry.

There is a certain potential in each person but it is developed by conscious effort, by aiming at being bigger and better than he normally is, not by preoccupying one's self with just getting by.

That's where Al-Anon's program is such a tremendous stimulation. No one could even half-live it without being a better person and, for those who really practice it in all their daily affairs, there is a satisfaction beyond physical comfort, a deep spiritual appreciation of true values and a mental ease which is Heaven itself after the turmoil in which we once permitted ourselves to live.

Practicing the 12 Steps perfectly is no little goal. It is a splendid and tremendous one at which to aim. And if Heaven is beyond our immediate grasp, in practicing the Steps as well as we are able, we catch glimpses of it which give new impetus to our search for serenity.

Arise and Walk

"Son, be of good cheer. Thy sins are forgiven thee . . . Arise and walk." These lines from Matthew (9, 1:8) come to us from nearly two thousand years ago but still they indicate priorities in Al-Anon. When the man "sick of the palsy" was brought before Christ, He "saw his faith and was moved to compassion." But which did He cure first, body or spirit?

And just as the paralytic's spiritual house was put in order before he was restored to physical health, so do we have to do in Al-Anon. If we simply go through the physical motions of the program by putting a curb unwillingly on our tongues, grudgingly feed the alcoholic, attend meetings only for the chance to complain or so that we may say, "I did *everything* I could," we are handicapping ourselves.

If an unfortunate situation endures very long, most of us show physical deterioration: insomnia, extreme nervous exhaustion, elevated blood pressure. Doctors help some but usually not enough. It is when some gleam penetrates our spiritual darkness, when we surmount our self-pity and resentment, when we "clean house," mentally and spiritually that we really begin to benefit from Al-Anon.

Along with shedding our spiritual trash, we lighten ourselves of an intolerable burden. Peace, serenity and acceptance follow so that we are released from crippling fears and can "arise and walk" with confidence and hope.

Gifts of Al-Anon

HOLIDAY TIME is a season of giving and all of us try to give gifts which will be useful, exciting, pleasing, welcome: gifts which will express our love.

That takes a lot of thought. We just can't walk into the first store we come to and, beginning with Anne at the top of our list, go right down to Warren, picking the first thing we see for each one.

"The gift without the giver is bare," and in this case our thought and our concern for exactly the right gift is a large part of the giver.

Fortunately Al-Anon's season extends through the whole year, through the whole world. And exactly the same qualities apply to Al-Anon's gifts. If we try to give another person hope and serenity, merely by mouthing its principles and slogans, our gift indeed is bare.

We have to give of ourselves: our experience, our methods and our conclusions. We have to give enough thought to what that other person has gone through, his feelings at the moment, and what will best help him glimpse his own capabilities, to enable us to choose exactly the right things to say to him.

We don't have to have golden words at our command. We don't have to be brilliant. We don't have to be wealthy in worldly goods.

We just have to care enough about Al-Anon and that "other" person, truly to give of ourselves. We have received Al-Anon's gifts in abundance. Let us bestow them with love, for it is our precious opportunity to help make the world a lot better for having had these gifts ourselves. "God bless us every one," and happy holidays to all.

From Me, to You, with Love

Father, help me to face issues, not to avoid them for fear of what others may say. Let me be willing to take risks, let me not be afraid of blunders. Give me courage to speak, even when I know I shall do it badly, and let me always believe in laughter as the solvent for self-pity. I pray also for grace to suffer fools gladly, especially that one which is myself. From "Prayers for a Busy Day."

What better way is there to begin a new year than with a prayer such as the one above? It is my New Year's gift to you. I hope you find in it all the things we in Al-Anon so frequently need, so badly.

It might almost seem that this prayer had been written for Al-Anon, for people like you and me who have so often shunted disagreeable issues around in our minds, afraid to face them and to settle them; afraid of risks, of mistakes, afraid of everything, in fact.

And even after we have been in Al-Anon for some time, many of us are still afraid to speak, exactly as the prayer says, because "I know I shall do it badly."

What if we make no hit at first? Polished oratory is not

expected at Al-Anon. If we don't make every intended point, in our first attempt, but have courage to try again, then we'll do better for having pulled ourselves together, put more thought on it, and got up and given it.

Laughter we find in Al-Anon, just as soon as we relax a bit and regain our perspective. And tolerance for suffering fools gladly is everywhere about us; we just have to learn to save a little for ourselves.

With or without this prayer, may you find serenity and happiness in the new year.

Patience Is a Virtue—and a Goal

EPITAPHS SEEM to have gone out of style. Folks settle now for just names and dates. But some of the old ones are well worth pondering. Take for instance, "Here lies a patient man." At first thought that doesn't seem like very much to say of a whole lifetime of living.

But think for a moment. Just what goes into patience? Surely it's not just gritting one's teeth and bearing discomfort, not just putting up with dullness, not just lulling one's self into a soothing stupor.

Patience is made up of much more: faith, hope, love, courage.

Without faith and hope, few of us could bear to contemplate tomorrow. This was just as true when Columbus sought a new route to the Indies as it is today, when we seek freedom from the H-bomb threat.

Without love, man wouldn't be bothered with anything but himself. Why should he be, if nothing means anything to him?

And certainly courage is a big part of patience: courage

to go on when life is difficult; courage to accept disappointment; courage just to go on being one's self, even in a humdrum way.

Patience is far from the negative virtue it seems at first. To have patience really is an all-time job, an all-day job, an every day goal to aim at. When we consider God's patience with us and our nonsense, we should be filled with determination to be more patient with Him and with our "neighbors"—and with ourselves!

Look Around You

EACH OF US needs something bigger than ourself to fall back upon, to carry us through each day. That's a cliché, but just pause and realize how true it is. Clichés ARE clichés because they represent universal experience.

It's not accidental that people speak of being down in the dumps or up on a cloud—most of us are exhilarated by heights and depressed by depths.

The fortunate ones among us find the something bigger within themselves: a spiritual outlook, a philosophy of life which carries them through. The others could, if they looked searchingly enough, find inspiration all about them.

During World War II we were stationed on an Air Base in Nebraska. The vast, level prairies drove some of our friends nearly out of their minds. They deplored the dreariness, the monotony.

But I loved the prairies. There was something exciting about being able to see all the way to the horizon, across land as flat as the runways. It was thrilling to look up to a sky as big as the earth, with not even a corner cut off by hills, nor hemmed in by buildings. The endless vista stirred my imagination and lifted my spirits.

Even in man-made New York there are things that lift the spirit, catch at the throat. Turn a corner and there's a church steeple with a single star hanging beside it; there's the sweep of a wide avenue in the rain with the glistening reflection of a thousand street lamps.

No matter where you are, you don't have to search for the something bigger within yourself, especially when you are unhappy. Look around you. Find something to make you stretch yourself, reach out of yourself. The lift it gives, and the peace it leaves, will carry you through the day.

We Need Your Thought, Help and Prayers

THIS APRIL FORUM begins with our soon-to-be-held World Service Conference, and it is ending with it, which does not really mean that we're going in circles at Headquarters. It simply indicates just how important is this phase of our development.

There was a time when Al-Anon was small enough and close enough for us to keep in touch with each other by means of what we called the "Clearing House." We tried to make that group as representative as possible, as interested in Al-Anon and as dedicated to its growth and perpetuation as we could. But groups then numbered less than a hundred and our world-impact was a lone group in England. Today we have not too many less than two thousand groups, all over the map, all with problems, all with interest in Al-Anon, all of them made up of individuals with a common, unhappy experience.

Like AA, in which we have our roots, one of our most

cherished beliefs is that the individual and the groups have the right to take what is wanted from the program. Every group is autonomous; every member's opinion is his own. We believe the less organization we have, the better it is.

These things we believe and cherish dearly. But we also are concerned that Al-Anon will endure. We see that, left to themselves, some groups may so change our program to suit themselves and to meet present (and perhaps transient) needs, that all Al-Anon may be affected: diluted, altered and hamstrung.

It is because we feel so heartily that Al-Anon must remain universal, cohesive and strong, that we are broadening the influence of those who guide it. The "group conscience" we so greatly rely upon must be as representative as possible, as broad as we can make it.

So, as we begin our Second World Service Conference, we need your help, your thoughts and your prayers for its success. We count on you, all over the world, to armor us as we meet.

Death and Taxes

THE LAST PLACE I would expect to find Oliver Wendell Holmes is on Uncle's Income Tax material. But there he is: "Taxes are what we pay for civilized society."

Probably because I was deep in producing the FORUM, the idea jumped into my mind that this also applied to us in Al-Anon. No one likes to pay taxes; very likely we'd all avoid them if we could. But we do enjoy the civilized society which results from their payment.

So, to the Al-Anon application of this principle: given a free choice, I believe few among us would have chosen an alcoholic problem with which to live. Left to ourselves, we'd rather have had a tranquil life in sunny places. But what would it have been? Few of us are like Jack's beanstalk which sprang up miraculously. We have to grow, most of us slowly. And we can't grow without challenge.

By ourselves, most of us made a mess of our reactions and relationships. It took Al-Anon's teachings and philosophy to straighten us out; it took coping with our problem through the Al-Anon program to stretch us spiritually, make us understanding and accepting.

If that is the price we had to pay, the tax required to keep us from the moral death of smugness, then the civilized society we now have in our homes and hearts is worth it.

Problems Make Progress

PEOPLE WRITE Headquarters or the FORUM for help on problems, either personal or group. Sometimes they recognize these as growing pains and sometimes there is vast impatience that not all is perfect.

Happily the ones who do recognize unresolved conflict as a step in development already have won half their battle. That is, if they are willing to be unselfishly ready for whatever solution is best for all concerned.

To insist on one's own panacea, simply because it is one's own, often leads from conflict to open warfare.

Growing pains are part of normal development. Not all of us are conscious of physical growing pains but such conditions exist. We frequently do not recognize unhappy experiences or set-backs as spiritual growing pains. But pains or problems, if accepted rightly, do contribute to spiritual growth.

People who coast along, sliding through life without

allowing themselves to become involved in anything, seldom if ever develop great moral stamina.

It's about the same physically. Take my daughter for instance. When she was little, she had spent most of her life on a Montana ranch, in pure mountain air and glorious sunshine.

Then at four, we visited Chicago and Buffalo one winter. She immediately began a series of critical illnesses. I was wild. I stormed at the doctor, told him of her ideal background and could not understand why this had not protected her.

Naturally it hadn't, he told me. She'd never been exposed to anything and so had never built up any immunity against anything.

Thus, if you do have problems, personal or group, keep on writing us. We may be able to help. We'll surely try. But please remember that problems can make progress.

Words To Live By

IN A Chinese Fortune cooky I found the lines, "Fear of danger is ten thousand times more terrifying than danger itself."

Immediately I thought of myself in early Al-Anon days and of the hundreds of newcomers to our program who spend countless days and endless nights tortured by infinite fears.

I couldn't define them, exactly, nor can these newcomers. There never was time to think—I just spent it being afraid. Everything milled around in my mind until the line between sanity and insanity thinned to a thread, and a cob-webby one at that.

Fortunately for me the Serenity Prayer gave me my

answer. I could not ask for courage to change the things I could change unless I knew which things they were. I couldn't accept those I couldn't change, either, unless I had the wisdom to know the difference. And there was no wisdom in my uncontrolled spinning from one fear to another. I had to sort out and distinguish which was which.

In that process of sorting, I had to face my fears. From an instinctive pushing aside of something nebulous but horrible, something I'd rather not think about, I had to dig out and bring to light just exactly what kept me in chaos.

When I did this, I found the serenity (patches of it) which comes from acknowledging the worst. At absolute rock bottom, any place else is UP.

Once on the way up, I could help myself rise higher, just as I could allow myself to slip back. At that point "Just For Today" was invaluable: "Just for today I will not be afraid." Sometimes "Just for this minute I will not be afraid" got me by some bad spots.

Thus serenity grew and flourished.

Gradually I reached the point where I could realize that "Fear of danger is ten thousand times more terrifying then danger itself." I didn't put it in those words but they surely rang a bell for me when I read them recently. They are words to live by.

"Be Still, and Know That I Am God"

IT'S SAID that many of us dig our graves with our teeth. I say that many of us make a hell for ourselves with our tongues.

We speak too quickly. When someone hurts us, we lash back. When it is life itself which hurts us, we fly apart. We're like dogs, chasing our tails, going nowhere fast, with each circle getting tighter. It takes almost a miracle to bring us back to reason.

Those of us living with the problem of alcoholism are fortunate because we do have a miracle to restore us to reason. We have guide-posts which already have helped thousands, to show us the way.

Ours is a program which demands thought. We have to weigh the past, learn from it, determine to benefit from it. We cannot do this successfully if we indulge ourselves in mental tantrums. We cannot do it all by ourselves. We need our fellow members and we need our Higher Power.

We know that the Higher Power has helped millions, is only waiting to help us. We are the break in the circuit, with our turmoil, our "alarums and excursions." Instead of frantically losing control when difficulties beset us, we should heed the psalmist: "Be still, and know that I am God."

Acceptance

WE IN AL-ANON are greatly blessed by the support we get from the Al-Anon program. From it we learn which things we can change, which things we must accept. We learn that a Higher Power is always at hand to ease our way. It is our privilege to spread the word of this philosophy not only to our children but to everyone with our problem.

My youth would surely have been less difficult had I been taught acceptance earlier. Nothing could change the fact that I followed immediately after a brilliant sister. I was not stupid, just average. But I came so close after my sister's shiny brains that teachers, accustomed to Mary's brilliance and expecting the same of me, put me down as mentally lazy. It infuriated me. I knew I was doing almost as well as I could and was being discounted.

One typical instance was our mutual French teacher. She cherished Mary's reply and broadcast it freely when the junior class was asked to define a gentleman. "One who acts, always, as if he were in the presence of God," said Mary without hesitation.

I, a freshman, recognized that definition as something pretty fine although then I'd have hesitated to talk so freely about God. I also recognized such an idea would never have crossed my mind.

But Mademoiselle vainly spent the next three years like a cat at a mousehole, waiting for me to come up with an equal gem.

Sixteen years of trailing after such clouds of glory left their mark on me. I rebelled and I resented. But I could not change the situation nor did I know enough to accept it.

Perhaps my stormy background accounts for my great reliance upon our prayer. One of Al-Anon's finest blessings and biggest helps is, "God grant me the Serenity to accept the things I cannot change, the Courage to change the things I can, and Wisdom to know the difference."

"As a Man Thinketh . . ."

IF YOU HAD a dollar for each time you've heard, "As a man thinketh, so is he," how far would they take you? I believe my dollars would take me clear to the Chinese Wall! There's something about thinking, however, which has no IF about it. Thinking can change one from a quivering mess of fear, a prey to every vagrant dread, into a well-adjusted, valuable person.

Many of us in Al-Anon fortunately have experienced such a change. And every one of us, even when new in Al-Anon, have seen it happen to others. Frequently the change came while a member was still living with an active alcoholic . . . and the only thing different about the situation was the mental attitude of the Al-Anoner.

No magic button will bring about this change, although the change itself is magical. It's accomplished through discipline, mental and spiritual.

It comes through a refusal to remain on the old treadmill of fear, worry and doubt. Actually it is a deliberate choice to put one's self into the hands of the Higher Power; to stop living in the unhappy past; to determine to "change the things we can."

Newcomers, perhaps, can accomplish only a moment of such positive thinking. But each moment is an entering wedge and the next one comes more easily. Added together, those precious moments soon become hours—days—and always. One's mind moves out of the squirrel-cage of worry on to an open road which leads out of difficulty . . . "As a man thinketh . . ."

Special Christmas Wishes

"JOY TO THE WORLD," "Oh Come, All Ye Faithful," "The First Noel," no matter how many times we've heard these carols, they always bring a catch at the throat, a quiet, inner thrill. Something about the Christmas season makes every happiness happier. But that same something deepens sadness if we are troubled.

And, over the years, many of us have been troubled at

this season. Christmas cheer had been too cheery for our loved one and our house too filled with spirits instead of spirit. If you are among those in distress today, take heart. What if you have to be Father and Mother Christmas both? What if you, unaccustomedly, have to carve the Christmas turkey? Most of us have done it. And survived.

But, if you are in Al-Anon, you have hope. You know that alcoholism is a disease, not a disgrace. You know that AA has worked its miraculous change in well over 300,000 —why shouldn't it work for your partner? Even if AA is resisted now, it may not always be.

Should such a Christmas ever again come to our house, I believe I would say to myself, "I'll be like Scarlett O'Hara in Gone With the Wind—I'll worry about it tomorrow." And I hope I would detach myself enough from the turmoil so that some of the Christmas spirit would conquer the sadness.

I deeply hope none of us has a less-than-perfect Christmas. But if, unhappily, this is not true for all, my special Christmas thoughts and prayers will be with the troubled ones.

The Wonder of Al-Anon

HAVE YOU EVER marveled at the power of Al-Anon to attract and to hold persons of such varying backgrounds: ages, races, creeds and stations in life?

A very powerful religion frequently does this. But Al-Anon is not a religious organization. We do believe in a "Power greater than ourselves" but each of us may relate that greater power to whatever he chooses.

I find it natural to think of this greater power as God

and, through the appropriate Steps, have been able to come closer to Him and at times to sense His will for me.

But in various groups with which I have been associated, I have known others who were completely agnostic and some even were atheists. They had success with the program, too.

One substituted the group conscience as her greater power, another used "all outdoors" as more powerful, while a third thought of a Diesel locomotive as a higher power.

Although none of these concepts is religiously motivated, the three members holding to them could frequently give me glimpses into depths of the program which I had missed.

While Al-Anon is not a religious program, it definitely IS a spiritual one. We have no dogma nor doctrine to which we must subscribe. We are free to pick and choose what we wish from the various aids the program offers.

The emphasis is all spiritual in that it is centered upon discipline of self, upon self-improvement and growth, upon development of concern for others and practical ways to help them.

There is nothing in Al-Anon to shut anyone out—everything is centered on bringing people in. And the wonder of Al-Anon is that it keeps on doing just that: giving comfort, restoring confidence, and shedding light in dark places.

Each Day's Business

As I LOOK back, we children were very patient with our father. For such an old man (he was in his thirties and early forties) he knew an awful lot. He'd spend endless time taking us places we wanted to go, although they must have bored him stiff. So that it was only common politeness, when he occasionally philosophized, that we appeared to listen with respect—if not with understanding.

He was a doctor. As with all doctors, he occasionally met with death in his practice. It was at such times, I suppose, he used to say, "Never count on a deathbed repentance. The business of the dying is with dying. Live each day now, just as if it were your last and everything will take care of itself."

We were patient with such nonsense. We had to grow up to know what he was talking about. We had to grow up to know that probably he knew we'd have to, but that we'd remember. The particular bit about each day, and a lot of his other exhortations, I now recognize as simon-pure Al-Anon thinking.

EACH day is the ONLY day we have. And if there are things about ourselves we want to change, today is the day to change them, or at least to begin working on them.

If someone you know is in difficulties and a call would help, go pick up your phone: next week he might be in such deep sadness that you couldn't help then. A call today could lift him out of it.

If you have a debt of kindness to pay, pay it today, to the person to whom you owe it or to someone else in his place.

But do each day's business each day.

Loving Kindness

KINDNESS ISN'T ENOUGH—the Bible says we should show loving kindness. Yet how many of us do, habitually? Certainly we all rise to special occasions, when sympathy for someone shakes us out of our preoccupations, when illness occurs or disaster strikes.

But in our everyday associations, how well do we do?

How many times do we fly at the throat of our nearest and dearest for perhaps well-meant and well-deserved criticism of a friend, not a tenth as close to us as the one at whom we fly?

We're apt to call it being loyal, but real loyalty surely should be to those nearest and dearest.

Again, when we're tired and overwrought, do we let loose at the neighbors, our co-workers, or even upon utter strangers, or do we use the family as our safety-valve?

Perhaps you don't do those things. But, looking back, I know I have. It doesn't take a searching moral inventory to tell me that no stranger can ever be as exasperating as a close relative. But that is no excuse.

We are told we should be kind to one another. And the kind of kindness needed is loving-kindness.

Sharing in Al-Anon

FEW PERSONS, of themselves, are strong enough, wise enough, to spend years with an alcoholic problem without suffering marked personality changes. In spite of themselves, most become introverted, shy and distrustful of intimate contact with others.

Even after coming into Al-Anon, many of these people remain ill at ease and are afraid to talk in meetings, much less speak to groups. This is a great pity for they are missing the greatest blessing and the greatest help that Al-Anon can give. That is the gift of lightening another's load. As children we were taught it is more blessed to give than to receive. In Al-Anon we have opportunities for both and should train ourselves so that we can benefit from both.

In the beginning, at my very first Al-Anon meeting, a miracle happened to me: the burden of fear, superstition and shame which I had carried for years, was lifted by one of the speakers who could have been describing my life in her talk.

She gave me courage to change my thinking but it took months before I could talk to anyone about it. When I did gather up courage to do so, it was at an Open Meeting in Montclair, N.J. I found to my amazement that FOUR persons at that one meeting had carried my same load. That night they were released, as I had been, and got new courage, as I had.

It doesn't much matter where I talk—in the mid-west, in Prince Edward Island, here around New York or a few weeks ago in Washington to a large group of wonderful people—everywhere I go and every time I tell the miracle of my first meeting, I find that same miracle works for some one there.

Remembering the pit I had dug for myself, from which I had been lifted, I rejoice at spreading the word to another. I thank God for giving me courage to have told it the first time in Montclair. I learned that it's only the first time which is difficult and seemingly impossible.

This sharing of experience in Al-Anon is one of the greatest, most important parts of our program. I often wonder if we have any right to allow shyness, self-distrust or embarrassment to keep us from helping another, as I was helped? And as the dozens (I've lost track of the numbers by now) who carried my burden, were helped? It is frightening just the first time.

So, when there's an opportunity to share your experience, by all means do so. That's Al-Anon.

Looking at Lois

HAVE YOU EVER thought what you would most like to have said about you? I have. I don't spend my time in envy but I often think of something my husband said about Lois, one of the founders of our fellowship.

In Al-Anon's early days my nearest group was thirty miles away and held night meetings only. Jack had to go along to drive; since there was no AA meeting those nights, he attended ours. As sometimes happens, there were several meetings in a row which could have been dullish for an AA.

Driving up to the next meeting I said, "I'm sorry you're sort of trapped when meetings aren't interesting to you." He promptly remarked, "Never feel that. When I find my mind wandering, I just stop listening and look at Lois. I never tire of looking at her—her face shows so clearly how much she has put into life."

Then I remembered Lois' story: the early days of AA when their home was stuffed, from cellar to attic, with alcoholics in all stages of recovery; the long years of active work and travel with Bill as he went about the world on AA business; how, when AA first established its General Service Conference and Bill could relax a little, she had looked forward to relaxing with him. Not a chance.

On one of Bill's trips he had found many Family Groups and realized they needed some organization to foster their unity and growth. Who so logical and handy, as Lois, to do this fostering?

So, once again she was plunged into the middle of very hard work. But everyone who knows Lois also knows she didn't shirk, didn't even think of it as hard work, but as opportunity.

All this shines from her face—reflects how much she has "put into life."

When I am tempted to take an easy way out, refuse to do a job because I'd rather rest, I remember Jack looking at Lois, and I decide to give my own face a chance to show something besides closed eyes.

Wall or Bridge?

DID YOU EVER pass a field with a bunch of gophers sitting up like sentinels? The instant one saw or scented you, they all dove into their holes. Many of us in Al-Anon were just like those gophers.

At first we sat up and faced the world. But when something happened which we didn't like, we withdrew; we found a hole for ourselves and crawled in. Gradually, as unpleasantness followed unpleasantness, we increased our negative defense by building a wall about ourselves and the hole we hid in.

We overlooked or ignored the fact that we were making a bad situation infinitely worse. Actually our wall was not shutting out any unpleasantness. It was shutting unpleasantness in. It prevented other people from reaching us. It kept us in shadow instead of sunshine. It kept us turned in upon ourselves when we were far from being congenial company, even to ourselves.

No matter how we managed to reach Al-Anon under such adverse conditions, Al-Anon put a good-sized breach in that wall. We gathered courage to emerge momentarily through the breach, to grasp for Al-Anon's help. Gradually, through grasping for Al-Anon, we built a bridge out from behind our wall, out to other people, to normal living and to life. It was a bit shaky and infirm at first but as it grew stronger it became a two-way bridge from us to the world and from the world to us.

It seems madness to us now that once we chose to build a wall instead of a bridge. Because of the bridge we have built, we now can reach others who have not yet found the way.

Doors

WHAT'S ON THE other side of a door? Just think how many doors Al-Anon has opened for each of us!

The golden door—bright as a new day—which Al-Anon opens, is labeled Hope: hope for dreary creatures who too long have huddled outside in their own shackles.

That door to freedom was there all the time but we had held it shut tight, with resentment, self-pity and despair. We never gave a thought to what was beyond.

When we at last permitted Al-Anon to open the door of hope, we little realized the tremendous change it would make in our lives and in those around us.

We were content, at first, just to know we were no longer alone. It was a blessed relief to know others had worked through situations as desperate as ours. They showed that even where they had been slightly marred, they were not permanently damaged.

As we progressed, learned really to live our program, we underwent a change which, sooner or later, was noticed by our families.

Instead of keeping doors shut by bitterness, indignation and injured pride (a way which leads to madness) we learned to open them to understanding . . . understanding of ourselves and our mates.

Sometimes, even, because our Al-Anon door opened to

us, our partner sought the open door of AA. He saw the serenity we had gained through the Al-Anon program and wanted the help of AA for himself.

That bonus is not given to all of us. But working the program to the best of our ability does give us peace.

Al-Anon in Action

SUCH WONDERFUL THINGS happen in Al-Anon! Just a year ago we had a stupendous response to Ann Lander's mention of Al-Anon in her widely-read newspaper column. Her advice to a wife, concerned about her husband's excessive drinking, was to write Al-Anon Family Group Headquarters. That one brief mention brought in over six thousand cries for help. Who knows, perhaps some unhappy person is still keeping the article, trying to gather courage to write.

Then there is the request, recently received at the World Service Office, asking if the Chicago Alcoholic Treatment Center could reprint "Twenty Questions an Al-Anon May Ask Himself," from the June and July FORUMS. Naturally permission was given.

Who knows how far Marguerite G. A.'s questions will finally reach? Already they have spread from West Chester, Pa., via the FORUM, all over the world to our thousands of groups. And now that the Chicago Center is distributing them, those twenty questions may well bring countless hundreds more to seek Al-Anon's help.

Letters to the FORUM is another phase of Al-Anon which brings a similar glow to my heart. A note from Phyllis Q., of the Siuslaw Group, Florence, Oregon, reads: "I especially want to thank the FORUM for the saying, 'The only way to Push is with Prayer.' It rang a bell for me when I first read it and I use it many times every single day."

The FORUM can't take credit for anything but printing this item. Nearly two years ago, on page 6 of the November '61 FORUM, you'll find an item from Florence G., Wyandotte, Mich.:

"I've worked hard for our new group and feel frustrated when meetings remain small; I know, though, that as in so many other areas, the only way I can 'push' is with prayer."

Talk about casting a stone into the sea and spreading ripples to the ends of the earth—Al-Anon's a lot like that. Who knows when something you write may be the difference between despair and hope in another's life, ten thousand miles from you?

What real help are you keeping to yourself, when it might be working?

Al-Anon Gold

How LONG has it been since you've reread Al-Anon literature?

My face turned deep red recently when I got Helen B.'s (California's first WSC Delegate) letter in reply to my query about where I could find "Three Deadly Enemies." Because it had been several years since I'd read "Alcoholism The Family Disease," and because I'd always associated these enemies with the California tapes, I'd forgotten they'd been reprinted there.

Helen is far too fine a person to have answered, "How come you didn't know this?" She just sent me the mimeo'd sheet and mentioned in her note I could also find them in the pamphlet. She's quite a girl.

But naturally I did feel silly—and should have. It made

me wonder just what else I have been missing because I've let so much time go by without reviewing all our other booklets.

Al-Anon has a lot of literature. But people and groups are constantly clamoring for more. There'll be more. We have a splendid Literature Committee to produce it.

But is full use now made of what already exists? Or is it read once or twice and on to the next piece? Some part of one booklet may help in a given situation but months later, when that situation has changed, another part of that same piece may be a lifesaver in the new situation.

You would be well repaid by a thorough review of all our literature. It is full of golden nuggets. But gold is where you find it. To find it, you have to look.

"Fear Knocked at the Door—Faith Opened it"

According to ancient legend, The Plague went to Bagdad to kill five thousand people. Instead, fifty thousand died. When someone questioned him as to why he had slain so many, The Plague replied, "I killed five thousand, as I said I would. The others died of fright!"

Some of us are like those extra forty-five thousand. We don't actually kill ourselves from fright, but we do kill a lot of the best that is in us. We maim ourselves by fearing many things which just never happen.

By letting fear overwhelm us, we prevent ourselves from making sane and sensible plans to tackle life's problems.

Emerson says, "Do the thing you fear and the death of fear is certain." He doesn't say this is an easy thing to do. He doesn't say to wait a week, when you have more courage. He just says, "Do the thing you fear and the death of fear is certain."

If you fear heights, I doubt that Emerson would advise you to jump off a church steeple to overcome that fear. He'd be more apt to advise you to face up to your moral and spiritual fears: the inherent self-distrusts, shynesses and inhibitions which keep you from being your real self.

Take his advice and remember: "Fear knocked at the door. Faith opened it. And lo! there was no one there!"

Vaya con Dios

CHRISTMAS BRINGS special joy, prompts us to a thanksgiving we may overlook at other times. We are favored beyond calculation because the gifts of Al-Anon are ours.

Think for a minute of the chances against us: there are 5,000,000 alcoholics in the United States. Figuring an average of only 5 persons associated with each, means there are 25,000,000 in need of Al-Anon help in this country alone!

Fast as our growth has been, we still probably have not reached more than 25,000 to 40,000 *in the whole world.* What did we few do to deserve this good fortune? Do we truly deserve it?

We do if we try to practice the program in all our affairs. When we do, I believe we are like Enoch who "walked with God." How better can we spend our days than in such company? No matter what we call our Higher Power, we cannot help but stretch ourselves spiritually if we are to accompany that Higher Power in all our waking hours.

To me, that Higher Power has always been God. I've never had difficulty in accepting God as the Supreme Being—my difficulty has been to keep myself free enough of the frets and strains of living so that I, too, may "walk with God."

That's why I love letters from Arbutus, our first WSD from Texas, who always closes even hurried notes with "Vaya con Dios." I'm devoid of Spanish but I'm sure it means "Go with God" and my spirits lift and I'm 6 inches taller.

So, for all Al-Anon, all Alateen and all AA, everywhere, may I wish for you every blessing of Christmas and may we all "Go with God" every day of the years to come.

Today's the Day

NEW YEAR'S DAY, traditionally, is the day when most of us aim to begin turning ourselves into soft-winged, haloed creatures of another world. That we seldom, if ever, accomplish this completely is beside the point. New Year's Day is a day of beginning and any beginning of self-improvement is better than continued complacency.

As a child, this day was always disappointing to me. I seemed never to learn from experience. Just as I expected some magic to show me the line between Illinois, where I lived, and Wisconsin, where I visited, I expected a difference between December 31st and January 1st.

But it was always just another day; Wisconsin wasn't pink, either, as it was on the map, with a straight black line separating it from an orange Illinois. I knew Illinois was green, really, with lawns, fields and woods, but Wisconsin should have been pink. So New Year's Day should have been different, too.

Now that I try to live by Al-Anon principles, with the 24-hours-at-a-time uppermost, I know that any day is a good day to begin work on whatever keeps me from practicing Al-Anon perfectly. It is not necessary to wait until the turn of the year to begin to turn over a new leaf.

The twentieth day of May or the tenth of March are just as good as January first—it's the beginning that counts.

But because something of childhood lingers in all of us, in spite of there being no real difference, January 1st is a good day to put our resolves into action, to concentrate more consciously on what we know we should be doing to improve the quality of our Al-Anon practice. If we should fail at first, there's nothing to prevent our beginning all over again, even on January second or February fifteenth. The main thing is to keep at it, never to be discouraged nor disheartened.

Happy beginnings to all of us and blessed accomplishments in the year ahead!

Try It Again!

THE HEADING on a leaflet I recently received startled me: "Try It Again" and I thought of my early days in Al-Anon. I believe I learned to walk early but, fully adult and then some, it took me more than three years to learn the First Step so that I really practiced it. I wasn't consciously trying to run things. I just thought there were things which hadn't been tried which would influence my husband.

Others have different problems: some, especially those working on the pamphlet "Just For Today," have difficulty in establishing a working time-table; procrastination dogs their feet.

Still others, highly organized and themselves proficient, determine to keep hands off while newcomers fumble through situations which seem simple to them and they intervene, even though they had determined to remain apart and let the newer one learn by doing.

Older members who have allowed themselves to domi-

nate a group, may have decided to stand by on the side-
lines, giving moral support, suddenly find themselves
smack in the middle again, telling everyone what's what.

Discouraging, isn't it? Every time I stumbled on that
First Step I thought I had it conquered. It was discouraging to have to pick myself up and begin again.

This all flashed through my mind as I read the heading,
"Try It Again." And it seemed to me the most simon-pure
Al-Anon admonition. It's the perfect sequel to "Why Not
Try?"

No matter what your problem is, you'll never get any-
where with it until you try to overcome it, so "Why Not
Try?" And if you don't succeed immediately, "Try It
Again!"

A lot of us were brought up on the tale of Bruce and the
Spider. If it takes seventy-times-seven, and more, to succeed in what we're aiming at, at least we are still alive to
try the four hundred and ninety first time. Why not Try It
Again?

Al-Anon's Second Wind

SECOND WIND suggests to most people great physical effort—
a tired man running a long race, an exhausted horse
plodding along extra, painful miles, or a swimmer tired
seemingly beyond endurance, yet keeping on. That there
is such a phenomenon is unquestioned.

There is, however, a second wind other than physical
which we may not think of immediately. That is the
spiritual second wind which keeps us coping with situations almost beyond tolerance.

We are about ready to give up when, from somewhere,

something keeps us going. This spiritual second wind is not automatic. We can count on it only if we condition ourselves for it.

Al-Anon, better than anything else, gives a kindergarten, an elementary-school and a university-course in such conditioning. Our whole program is based upon the idea of working on ourselves.

Every part of Al-Anon philosophy is pointed toward self-improvement. And every good experience in Al-Anon helps us appreciate that, through Al-Anon, we have had a spiritual awakening which gives us the obligation to help others as we have been helped.

When we are tempted to give up, to let chaos, turmoil and sadness overwhelm us, our background in Al-Anon steps forward and gives us our second wind to keep us going.

We may not know it is there within us. But in time of need we discover it. We find we have the strength, the will, even the wish to carry on to victory over ourselves.

That spiritual second wind Al-Anon gives us is its most priceless gift—worth all the blood, sweat and tears it takes to attain it.

"Nothing to Fear but Fear"

Do you sit back at meetings, just listening, reluctant to give your opinion because you're shy? Do you hesitate to join the discussion because others seem to have better ideas to contribute?

If so, it's a pity. After all, similar as all our experiences have been, each learned a great deal from them and this knowledge really goes to work when it is shared.

The little extra twist you put on your interpretation of a Step or a slogan, might make just the difference in helping someone else understand it. Might make the difference between success and failure in his following that part.

Many of us come into Al-Anon not in complete control of ourselves. Either we are compulsively talkative or compulsively silent. Neither attitude is particularly good for the group, but the second is especially bad for the quiet one—no one knows quite how to help, because he doesn't know exactly where help is needed.

For your own sake try to contribute ideas and experiences. Begin in your own meeting and practice on the members. They aren't really a critical or formidable group, but just Al-Anon friends, there to help and be helped.

Then, when you're asked to talk elsewhere, don't draw in your horns, make excuses and refuse. That other group is just Al-Anon, too.

Speaking at meetings, large or small, is just 12th Step work on an extended basis. I believe if we all thought of it in this way and remembered that most of those in the audience are Al-Anons like ourselves, it wouldn't be difficult to get speakers.

There's a real challenge in speaking at meetings, especially large ones. There's also a tremendous thrill and reward.

A bit ago I spoke at the 5th Annual Al-Anon Rally in Detroit. I believe close to 700 were there. What did I have to give to so many different people? I have exactly what we all have—our own experience, and I gave my struggle with the First Step.

I'm sure no matter how hard I work on my talks, they are far from perfect. But they are honest, factual accounts of how I allowed a difficult experience to affect me, and how Al-Anon lifted me out of despair. No one else could give exactly that talk because no one else lived it and was affected by it.

And what a reward I had! Never was there a warmer, more generous welcome; never a more enthusiastic reception of an unknown out-of-towner; never did new friends seem like old friends so quickly. And this is always true.

So, if you are afraid to open your lips, remember that especially in Al-Anon, "We have nothing to fear but fear" when it comes to addressing meetings.

Stop! Look! Listen!

MOST OF TODAY'S roads are so built that old-fashioned level crossings of railway tracks are practically a thing of the past. And along with them have gone the Stop! Look! Listen! signs. I can't remember when I last saw one. Probably there are new, young members amongst us who've never seen one.

In a way that's too bad. We no longer need them with highways which cross railroad tracks on elevated bridges. But they would serve as valuable reminders for us to stop and think on certain occasions.

Too often, in impatient irritation, we sound off when it would be better if we stopped for even a moment's reflection.

If I seem to revert to this subject frequently, it's because so many of us do this so often. We seem opposed to learning better.

Naturally we can always admit regret when we do realize we've been wrong. But in the meantime we've set a chain reaction in motion—we have got ourselves upset; we have shown our displeasure, and because we did so as a result of too-hasty speech or of misunderstanding, the other person reacts adversely, and a mess results.

Probably all the unpleasantness could have been avoided had we not spoken so quickly—had we waited until we were thinking instead of speaking.

Stop! Look! Listen! signs, well distributed along all our mental paths and processes, might help all of us to calmer, friendlier, more peaceful lives. In winning friends and influencing people, they could be a decided asset.

If you've been having difficulty with others—naturally because *they* were wrong!—why not try a week of Stop! Look! and Listening, and see how much it helps.

Do It Now!

SOMETIMES IT TAKES a real jolt to shock us into an appreciation of just how important our twenty-four-hour program is. If we practiced it perfectly all the time, we'd act immediately on every good impulse we have. But all too often time presses at our heels and we move on to something else.

Such a shock came to me last week, with news of a Board member's husband's death. I'd always liked Jerry, especially after Adele told me he couldn't wait for the FORUM to come. He'd get home before she did, so he always read it first. She couldn't have it until he'd finished it.

One time, when I wrote a piece he particularly liked, he told her to kiss me for him. What editor could resist flattery like that?

I always planned to thank him personally for the nice things he said but we seldom met. When we did, very occasionally, it was at times like the Conference gathering at Lois's, or the picnic, where I'd be busy seeing people about the FORUM, and I'd think, "Next time I'll be more free and I'll stop then and really talk—thank him properly when I have time."

Now I have time. But Jerry isn't here to be thanked. Not that I believe he ever held neglect against me, or even thought of it. But it would be a comforting thought, since he is beyond me now, if I could remember having told him my delight in his appreciation of the FORUM.

Some good will come from all this, because I'll be more conscious of doing today's affairs today, of taking care of immediate concerns the moment the opportunity arises and not waiting for a better chance, which may not come.

Do it now is a good precept for me—and perhaps for you, also.

Understanding

PEOPLE ASK where ideas come from for the bits and pieces printed here. The answer is everywhere.

One piece I liked a lot came from the Income Tax form a year or so ago, where Oliver Wendell Holmes was quoted as saying, "Taxes are the price we pay for civilized society," and it made me think that living with an alcoholic was the price we paid for the really pricelsss gift of Al-Anon and we should see it in perspective.

Mystery stories have contained things which suggested ideas for many articles.

Since I read everything which comes within a mile of me, even matchbook covers, practically anything can suggest an article. July's comes from an Epilepsy Foundation stamp which read, "Understanding is half the treatment."

The French have a saying that "To understand all is to

forgive all," which always used to seem to come close to what our program does for us.

But now, thanks to the stamp, I believe "Understanding is half the treatment" really pinpoints it for us.

After years of trying unsuccessfully to take the First Step, and then finally making the goal, my resentment toward alcoholism finally waned. With that acomplishment behind me, there didn't seem any indication for "forgiveness."

With the First Step I knew the alcoholic was as powerless over alcohol as I, that it was a disease, so how did forgiveness enter? It seemed presumptuous to me even to think of it that way.

But understanding that it was a disease, a terrible compulsion beyond anything in normal comprehension, was the real beginning of my recovery. I don't know a single thing about the Epilepsy Foundation, except that they sent me stamps and I sent them a little money but I do know their slogan could well be Al-Anon's.

Why Are You in Al-Anon?

ARE YOU IN Al-Anon because someone said, "It's Al-Anon or else." Are you there to find a magic formula to dry up a consuming thirst? Are you there because life seemed too dusty to be worth while? Whatever the reason which drove you to seek help, you have found something in Al-Anon.

Even those who attend but one meeting get help, if nothing more than knowing others have had a like experience.

If you have stayed and have conscientiously worked the program, you have found a whole new way of life. This in spite of its being a "suggested" program only. No one tells you what to do. No one says you must do this to accomplish that.

Your own revulsion at your former attitude makes you reach eagerly for whatever it is which has made those others, with identical experience, so calm, serene and relaxed. You know that since they got it—and they show they have—you can get it too. All you have to do is to listen to them and learn.

One caution is necessary: Sir Winston Churchill has said it. He was a realist with the courage to say exactly what he meant. Remember when he told a desperate nation he could offer them nothing but "blood, sweat, tears and toil?"

He was equally realistic and uncompromising when he said, "It is no use saying, 'We are doing our best.' You have got to succeed in doing what is necessary."

We in Al-Anon have to succeed in doing what is necessary to regain our tranquility. We cannot be fair to ourselves, to our families, and to our responsibilities in life if we allow our problems—no matter how great nor how trying they are—to bog us down in a mess of quivering nerves.

If our best is not good enough, we have to concentrate on making it better. Help is ever-present in Al-Anon, even for the "loners," though that is the hard way to get it.

We fortunate ones in groups have an incomparably simpler time where we have successful examples always before us.

Let us never pause half-way with the false comfort of saying "We are doing our best." Let's dig in our heels, brace our shoulders and keep working until we have succeeded in doing what is necessary to become useful, attractive people again.

Don't Bury the Past too Deep

LUCY P. asked for my personal opinion on which is most helpful to an Al-Anon member: to try to close the door on the past or sometimes to look back on it?

If each of us is really the sum of his faults and virtues, the result of all his past, I personally don't believe we can ignore that past, just by waking up fresh each morning. That'd be fine but I don't see how it can be done.

If yesterday I stole a dollar from my neighbor, today I am a thief if I have not returned the money, acknowledged the theft and made amends.

But if I *have* made amends as far as is humanly possible, I do not have to live perpetually as yesterday's thief. I have made amends, can forgive myself and need to remember yesterday's fault only when tempted to commit the same error.

Most of us have done wrongs in the past at which we shudder, now that God has "restored us to sanity." Because I once hurled a priceless dish in a fit of uncontrolled anger, because I frequently yelled and screamed ugly, violent names and threats, I do not have to remember all of it in detail—go over it like a string of beads, each counting against me.

That was what I did then, when I knew no better and could do nothing else.

Now I do know better and I don't do those things. But since I have shoulder blades instead of wings, I am sometimes tempted to revert, and then it is well for me to remember that the past should teach me something. I did those things once; I cannot deny them.

I do not wish to repeat them. I can help prevent repetition by occasionally remembering how uncontroled I once was. I do not have to be the person I used to be and I do not have to allow the past to be a stone around my neck. After all, if I should sprout wings, it might impede their growth.

I just have to carry enough of the past along with me into my present so that it will help my future be fair and bright.

Something for You to Do!

THERE'S A LINE from the poet John Donne—the exact wording escapes me at the moment but the gist is, "I, a stranger and afraid, in a world I never made." That could be any of us. But we can't sit back and give up.

No generation of man ever is given the free choice of the problems which confront it; no individual ever really controls his future. He aims at it; he sometimes surmounts some difficulties. But there is always a residue, some flaw in himself or his surroundings, to cope with.

We in Al-Anon are fortunate that the flaw in our own surroundings is one which enables us to stretch out a helping hand, to give life-saving sanity to others now situated as we once were.

Had we not had the common background of alcoholism, we could never lead others to the acceptance we have gained.

God does not wait until we have attained perfection to use us for His purposes. He takes us as we are and enables us to share the serenity we have achieved with others who are still struggling.

The way is not always easy. I used to pass a gypsy fortune teller's studio with a sign in the window which read, "Come in and hear what you wish to hear." Always I used to think, "Wouldn't that be wonderful!"

But all the time I knew it was make-believe and the things which would help me to grow, and to mature (not just grow older) were things I *had* to hear . . . things like keeping hands off, living just one day at a time and allowing God's Will, not mine, to guide me.

If ever you are tempted to toss in the sponge and fall back upon the idea that it's "a world you never made," remember that of course you didn't make it but you don't have to leave it in the mess you found it.

You can't do much about many of the world's problems, but as long as there is one mate of one alcoholic in need of help, there's something for you to do. You've had a like experience, you have all of Al-Anon's tools—all you need do is use them, by sharing.

The Al-Anon Mail Bag

IF I COULD be granted just one wish for all Al-Anon, I think I might wish to have every member read one week's mail.

Naturally many letters are routine, taken for granted, like changes of address of secretaries. A lot is literature orders and notes enclosing contributions. But all show the Al-Anon spirit of helpfulness . . . groups keeping us posted so mail won't go astray.

I like to follow the literature orders mentally and think where they will eventually end up, and what power they will have to change lives. A piece sent to a group in New Mexico can well be forward-passed to South Africa!

I have written many times of the joy of speaking and the thrill which comes when my experience matches another's, and helps that person. This happened to me in Maryland a few weeks ago and makes that weekend an unforgettable one. When a woman in Detroit last spring said the most valuable part of my talk was when I said, detailing my efforts to control alcoholism before I took the First Step, "I did everything. The only thing I didn't do was do nothing." She'd been doing everything, too, but was going to do nothing from then on, except on herself. Delight, indeed!

But more rewarding even than that are the letters which come, desperate and frightened, asking for help and are followed a few months later with letters bubbling over with confidence and hope and thanks. Each of us in our group has had the same feelings when newcomers accept the program. This is a thrilling experience. But when it is multiplied a hundred times, through countless letters from all over the world, it catches at one's throat and softens one's heart.

Letters to the FORUM are especially precious because they all aim at helping someone. I wish I could print more. I wish most of all that all of you could read all of the mail—mine and Headquarters', both.

What's Wrong with Pollyanna?

HAVE YOU EVER gone through an entire day—granted you live among people and are not a reed, bending in the wilderness—without meeting one unhappy person? Or at least one person who *looked* as if he were unhappy?

Our little JUST FOR TODAY quotes Lincoln as saying that "Most folks are as happy as they make up their minds to be." So why shouldn't we make up our minds to be happy?

We're told (here I am not sure of my mathematics but I am of the idea) that it takes nineteen muscles to frown but only a dozen to smile. You'd think human inertia would make us smile more than frown. But few of us do.

"Just for today I will be happy." I'll make up my mind to be happy and then I shall be, along with Lincoln who went out of his way to lighten others' loads. If I have things to sadden me, and who hasn't, I'll think them over until I can find some good in them and I will not let them get me down.

One bus driver, who waits a moment for me to get aboard instead of slamming his door on my nose, one paper boy who smiles as he hands me my morning paper, can give me a lift for the day.

I can spread good will and good spirits by smiling as I hold a door open for the person behind me. If I smile, that person will smile back.

"Just for today I will be happy." If each of us plans this for each day of our lives, we'll see plenty of happy faces wherever we go and the blessings of the happy holiday season we all wish everyone will last far beyond Christmas and New Year's—we'll change our whole world. Christmas love to each of you.

Attitude of Gratitude

HOW MANY TIMES have you heard someone—usually a woman, widowed, with grown children or childless—say, "There's no one I have to please; no one I have to account to and no one to whom I owe anything. I can please myself."

But is this ever true? Certainly it is true of minor things—it doesn't matter if such a person chooses to eat on a tray instead of setting a formal place at a table. It is true it doesn't matter if she reads late and sleeps 'til nine o'clock.

If she had worn pastel colors all her married life when she really wanted bright ones, good for her if she goes out and buys fire-engine red shoes or a Kelly green dress. Surely both are harmless and quite satisfying.

It's this business of not owing anything to anyone which is impossible to justify. I do not believe it is reasonable that any person could reach mature years without owing something to someone—a kindness done, a thoughtful act in time of stress, a hope held out when things were dark.

I know that one can't continue to thank someone endlessly for a kindness done. But one can continue to be thankful that it was done and to look around for ways to express that thankfulness.

In our fellowship no one need look far to find someone still in need. Lifting that person's spirits with a thoughtful word or a kind act is a small payment on one's own debt.

Should you ever catch yourself saying, or thinking, "I owe nothing to anyone," stop and really think. Don't dwell on the bitter disappointments—concentrate on who and what helped you overcome them.

Don't count the hurts you have received but remember the kindnesses extended you—and repay them tenfold to anyone still in need. It is this ability to scatter blessings in recognition of blessings we ourselves have received, which makes us persons worth knowing and having as friends.

Be Generous with Your Past

LARGE NUMBERS of letters come to the FORUM, which is natural and good. Ten times the number would be heartily welcomed. But one thing is strange and it happens quite frequently: months or maybe years will pass without a single letter on a given subject. Then, out of the blue will come three, four or a dozen, from places as widely scattered as it is possible to be, all on the same subject.

In the past few weeks these multiple letters have been about fear of speaking to groups. This is something which concerns us all, because group meetings are an important part of our program. We need speakers for them, speakers who are willing to stand up and tell their own experiences, before and after the program.

Granted that some people are more shy than others, that it is difficult for them to address more than two people at once, that they prefer to remain in the background and do their share by washing cups or straightening up after meetings—both necessary jobs. Ask yourself if this is enough.

One of these recent letters shows a self-analysis which goes deeper than the others. This writer says she is, and always has been, afraid to speak in public. She pondered and came up with the reason that she was "afraid of making a fool of herself." Once she established that reason, she set to work to overcome that fear. Little by little she is training herself to talk to more people and I am sure it won't be long before she is addressing larger groups successfully. What has she got that you don't have?

I, myself, have as wild and silly a story as anyone possibly could have. I was so far gone I seriously asked a surgeon to break my husband's leg so he'd be immobilized and I could, Gorgon-like, keep him from going out after liquor. That doesn't show much sense—and I didn't have much—but my telling it has helped a lot of people feel they weren't too bad . . . they didn't slip back that far from the norm.

When one is seriously questioning his sanity, it is real

comfort to know that someone else, now apparently in full possession of himself, had gone farther off the rails than he, but still came back to sanity. How can anyone ever know this if no one speaks and says it?

There are a lot better speakers in Al-Anon than I am. But I am the only one who can tell *my* story. I am the only one who had my particular battle with the First Step. If some member still is having difficulty, after struggling six months with it, it is reassuring to hear that I fought four years to take it successfully. But I finally made it, and the whole program fell into place. Who else can tell them that? And if I do tell them, and someone in the audience is still fighting it, does it matter if I am not a silver-tongued orator? That person gets the message all right, and very likely his battle is cut short by months or perhaps a year.

My correspondent who analyzed her reluctance to speak in public as being caused by fear of making a fool of herself was very wise. I am sure it is fear of failure which ties her tongue. But why should she be afraid? We are all Al-Anons, one or five hundred of us. Each of us has a unique experience, enough like someone else's to help that person. But we have to share it. We have to tell it because it is our story and no one else can tell it.

Many people are helped just by looking around a group, seeing happy faces, and realizing members can laugh at themselves. But many more are given a tremendous lift when they hear a story like their own which ends successfully. But they have to hear it—they can't get it by osmosis. Don't let pride, fear or shyness keep it from them. Those three qualities are enemies of our program. Be generous with your past—someone needs it more than you!

"Time to Stand"

> A poor life this, if full of care
> We have no time to stand and stare.

W. H. Davies wrote that. I wish I had. I believe each of us has an extra moment in the day to flex spiritual muscles or to take a bit of time out.

I'm sure, no matter how busy each of us is, we could pause a minute and think of something wholly detached from ourselves, and we'd be better for it.

When one is living with an active alcoholic, all too often there are pressing financial problems. These are real and important. I have heard people say, *"I* know alcoholism is an illness, but does my landlord? Will he wait?" And all day and far into the night they are haunted by the thought of what they will do for the rent.

Still others slog through each day, trying to do the impossible of keeping up with a family and a house which is too much for one alone. All day they say to themselves, "As soon as I wash the clothes I'll scrub the kitchen but when can I get at last week's darning?"

They are all so oppressed by the burden of the moment, real as it is, they never get a second's refreshment. Handicapped by a serious problem to begin with, that problem is soon aggravated out of all proportion.

It would be better, instead of eternally running on this vicious treadmill, if one pulled himself up short and said:

"Look, now, that is enough nonsense for a while. Put every worry out of your cluttered mind and think for two minutes of the nicest thing that ever happened to you—or of the most peaceful place you've ever been."

Don't allow yourself to get trapped into self-pity that the nice thing isn't happening now, nor that you aren't in that peaceful place. Just live it over again and relax in it.

There's little that is new in this idea. But it does have authority behind it. Nearly two thousand years ago when Christ walked the earth, He dropped in to see two sisters. One sat and drank up His wisdom and inspiration. The other scurried from pot to pan, hastened to tidy up for Him and got herself in a stew so that she soon complained to Him that Mary just sat and listened and left all the work to her.

He listened and agreed. But, He said, "Mary has chosen the better part and it shall not be taken from her." After all, He was the first to say that man did not live by bread alone and He put spiritual things first.

Nobody knows better than I that the hours of the day and the night are not made of rubber. But as I walk along a city street, I *can* look up and see a jet streak across the sky; I can pause a second and watch a flock of pigeons swoop and wheel, just for the joy of movement.

If I'm on a crowded bus, I can think myself back to a Montana meadow strewn with a million wild flowers. I can see whole ranges of glorious mountains, the white-on-white of their rugged snowcapped crests sharp against the clouds behind them. I can reflect that those mountains were there before a man lived to see them.

Instead of the squirrel cage I used to spin in, I now take time to stand and stare. And I'm happier and better for it.

Testimonial to March's "Time to Stand"

As EVERYONE well knows who has ever heard me speak, who has read more than ten lines I have written, and who has talked five minutes with me about Al-Anon, I had the greatest difficulty with the First Step. When I finally was able to accept it, the whole program fell into place and I have since tried to practice it in all my daily affairs.

I had a real test recently of practicing what I preach—although I do hope I don't sound preachy.

Just as I was finishing up the March FORUM at the end of January, I had a most horrifying experience. In elegant New Yorkese, I was "mugged" by two young men in the lobby of my building, shortly after six in the evening.

One held me, helpless, while the other snatched my handbag. My right middle finger was broken. Pain and shock later made sleep a bit difficult.

That first night I did take a capsule the doctor prescribed but my mental state was such that the medicine couldn't relax me. Every time I closed my eyes I felt that arm come from behind, crushing my mouth and holding me helpless. I'd shiver and shake and get the horrors. If ever anyone was on a vicious treadmill, I was. Then I suddenly remembered a "Time to Stand" I'd written so recently.

My first thought was, "you certainly are a dandy to give help to anybody. Why don't you take your own advice?"

Within moments, I felt myself back in Montana in the springtime with my daughter. We'd have to watch where we put our feet as we crossed meadows and pastures, so that we'd step on the fewest wild flowers. There were so many millions of them we felt free to pick some. So I set myself mentally to gathering Mariposa lilies, fritillarias, moccasin flowers, lady-slippers and countless others. I still couldn't sleep but I could relax and did.

Every time the thought of that terrifying experience tried to creep back into my mind I instantly thought of Montana's peace and quiet—either the dramatic springs, the satisfying summers or the marvelous winters with mile upon mile of spotless snow.

In a week's time, the awful thoughts stopped coming while I was conscious. And it has been two weeks since I woke my husband up by screaming in my sleep—I'm working on my subconscious now and having some success, apparently.

I don't recommend going through such an experience to prove a point—even one of my own—and the things I've suggested before have always been ones I'd already tried and proved successful.

But the fear and anxiety I'd known previously were child's play to the horror and terror, the physical indignity and all the rest incidental to this mugging. What worked in such circumstances will work in others equally serious.

There's nothing like taking time to "stand and stare."

In the Presence of God

A MOST IMPORTANT part of our program reminds us that we have only today with which to concern ourselves . . . only right now, in fact.

For many of us, blotting out the past is a tremendous comfort. We are not proud of past performances; we know we sometimes were tried beyond endurance but also know we let off steam many times on the nearest person, frequently on our children who had done nothing to deserve the wrath poured out on them.

If we did no lasting harm to them, and fortunately few of us did, it was because they instinctively knew we were not really ourselves, and thus bore no malice. They came out of the ugly picture better than we.

Blotting out the past is good; it is healthy not to brood over it. But enough of it should be remembered to prevent us from ever falling into the same error again.

I've written this incident before but you can see the

impression it made on me. When we were very young, my older sister had her own definition of a gentleman: one who acts always as if he were in the presence of God.

That's quite a definition for a sixteen-year-old to think up herself and I've never forgotten it. I believe most of us want to consider ourselves ladies and gentlemen. If we live by Mary's definition, we'll have no occasion ever to be sorry for the things we do.

If God were visibly present, I cannot imagine any of us venting impatience on innocent heads. It is hard to imagine any impatience at all in such a Presence.

Thus, when trials come (and what life is without some?), Mary's definition is a sheet anchor, and I gladly share it now with anyone in need.

"This Is the Day—"

"THIS IS THE DAY which the Lord hath made." The psalm is one of thanksgiving and while it indicates difficulties and enemies, they are already vanquished and the general theme is of rejoicing.

All too often we quote this line on bright, perfect days, when everything is going well for us. We feel it goes with such days, but how about dark, troubled ones? God made those days too—in fact He makes all days and has been doing it for a long time so there's little that's accidental about them.

If we could learn to accept trials, setbacks, and disappointments as part of the days that God hath made, we'd begin to gain perspective.

We know nothing is going to last forever. We know we must have something to overcome, to pit ourselves against, if we are to grow and become strong. We don't develop character licking marshmallows.

When we learn to take the bad, as well as the good, in stride, then we have begun to mature, to become persons worth having for friends, ones upon whom others can count.

Those who are a mile in the air today, and sunk in the depths tomorrow, are not much good to themselves nor to anyone else.

It's not written anywhere that just good things should happen to us. We need checks, restraints and postponements, as well as rewards and satisfactions.

Let's recognize that today—and every day—is the day that God hath made and derive some good from it, rejoicing.

Joy in Al-Anon

IN THE PAST few weeks, as this is written, several hundred letters have come to Headquarters in response to a mention of Al-Anon in a syndicated article. It was my privilege to handle 60 or 70 of these letters because I can again be a regular volunteer at the World Service Office.

Things are different there now. Twelve years ago, before my USO job, when cries for help came we were delighted to be able to refer inquirers to groups a hundred miles or more away. All-too-often groups were five hundred miles away and all help had to be given by correspondence.

It was a joyful surprise, when I counted up and found that more than half the inquiries came from persons in towns where an Al-Anon group was already established. Of the balance, most came from persons within forty miles of a group, and with today's transportation, that is not a hopeless distance. What a joy to tell those people how near at hand there was personal help for them!

And in that same period a letter came from Horicon, Wis., saying their group had had growing pains, problems, etc., and had dropped from a large group to only two. Those two, however, had kept on with regular meetings, reading and discussing Al-Anon topics. To their delight two new members had just joined them, overwhelmed with gratitude for finding help.

Marie wrote: "I felt like crying but held the tears back as I knew I must give them understanding, not sympathy. How very important it is to remember that even if a group dwindles to just a few members, those members should not give up. I thank God that Betty and I decided to keep a light burning lest a troubled person was seeking what we had been privileged to find."

Thank God for such a spirit in keeping a group alive, and thank God for all the other groups for being there to reach out a helping hand to those in need. We are indeed blessed.

Sermons in Stones

JUST A WEEK AGO, at noontime, one of our group telephoned me to say it was impossible for the one who was to lead the meeting to be present. Would I pinch-hit?

I am a newcomer to the group because it is a daytime meeting and while I was working I could not attend. Of course I accepted. Since there hadn't been a Tradition meeting in the months of my attendance, I read them and very lightly outlined what they meant to me. This was well received.

Then, as it is a discussion group, I asked if there were any newcomers or anyone who wished to talk about anything. One woman spoke up and said she was desperate, was thinking of leaving her husband or doing something drastic to herself. We told her we could give no marital counseling but we did give her a resumé of our own experience.

Everything we suggested that had worked for us was countered with the flat statement that her case was different or she'd already tried it. It was sort of a hopeless situation because her mind was tight shut, yet she obviously needed help desperately.

I went home rather depressed, the meeting a stone in my heart. I felt I'd led the meeting and should have found some acceptable answer for her.

My husband came home and sensed my worry, so I told him of having failed completely to reach a woman and that it bothered me because I had chaired the meeting. Naturally I said only that a woman had come for help and had not got it, although every person there had tried her best to give it.

He thought a minute and then said, "You shouldn't let it get you down. Something that was said may reach her later. And even if it doesn't, you said every member of the group tried to help and did their best. It's tough you couldn't reach her but the meeting wasn't wasted: every member there benefited from trying."

Then Shakespeare's lines from "As You Like It" popped into my head:

> *Sweet are the uses of adversity;*
> *Which, like the toad, ugly and venomous,*
> *Wears yet a precious jewel in his head;*
> *And this our life, exempt from public haunt,*
> *Finds tongues in trees, books in the running brooks,*
> *Sermons in stones, and good in every thing.*

That meeting *was* a stone to me but there *was* good in it, although, in my disappointment, it had to be pointed out to me.

A Bug's and a Bird's Eye View

IF WE TAKE a good look at what Al-Anon has done for us, most of us see that we, personally, have gained greatly. From gibbering, hagridden, craven cowards, a close look at ourselves shows we've gained courage, confidence and a more-or-less-great measure of serenity.

That is quite an impressive accomplishment for a program, itself purely voluntary and suggested, to achieve. It is one which has no do's or don't's in it, other than keeping an open mind. It leaves acceptance wholly to each individual.

Any program which accomplishes this can stand on the record alone. But take a moment to think, how much *more* Al-Anon does. Good wrought in its members never stops there. It spreads far and wide into all personal relationships, to the families and to the community.

When a frightened, insecure, immature person really accepts what Al-Anon can give, when he faithfully practices the program in all his daily affairs, that person stops holding himself as the exact center of the universe. He stops fighting battles which are not his to fight. He concentrates on actions where he has a chance to win. He relaxes enough so that he can again think of others and can again make a normal contribution to his home, church and community.

No outsider ever can say which home should be broken and which should stand. But Al-Anon has saved many and many a home from being broken.

Al-Anon has helped countless children regain respect for

their alcoholic parent, not only through teaching that alcoholism is a disease but by the changed attitude of the non-alcoholic. It has prevented numberless children from ever losing this respect through the same teaching.

It has changed many a home from a cat-and-dog kennel back to a home where there is acceptance, compassion and love.

So, if ever you become discouraged by a bug's eye view of your own progress in Al-Anon, be patient with yourself. Try a little harder. Remember what you were in pre-Al-Anon days. Countless others before you have freed themselves of daily, mundane failure in understanding, have risen above all of it, to get a bird's eye view of ultimate success.

What has been done, *you* can do. And it's worth the unhappiness along the way. After all, how many people can change themselves from cowering wrecks into valuable citizens? Through Al-Anon, you can.

Alice and Al-Anon

AL-ANON MEETINGS frequently remind me of The Mad Tea Party. They are very like and very different: "You should say what you mean," the March Hare said to Alice.

"I do," Alice hastily replied; "at least—at least I mean what I say—that's the same thing, you know."

"Not the same thing a bit!", said the Hatter, "Why, you might just as well say that 'I see what I eat' is the same thing as 'I eat what I see!' "

"You might just as well say," added the March Hare, "that 'I like what I get' is the same thing as 'I get what I like!' "

Many Al-Anon members are living with a still active

problem of alcoholism, which is not like Alice's Wonderland but certainly is just as topsy-turvy. In my own group I believe more than half the membership is numbered here. But, like Alice, they are trying to understand and make themselves understood under difficult circumstances.

The greatest and the most rewarding thing of our meetings is that we meet with a *willingness* to understand. No one barks at us "to say what we mean" if we have phrased something badly. Members take time and trouble to sort out the underlying meaning.

Best of all, our meetings are a place where we can say anything about anything which is troubling us, without having to wonder three times if it will touch off an adverse reaction. That is of priceless value to anyone living with a nervous, resentful partner still fighting a violent battle within himself.

When a situation resolves itself, as it usually does sooner or later when real serenity is attained, this freedom of speech is not as essential as in the early days. But it is always welcome. Some newcomers never say anything at all for months on end. But all the time they are absorbing the relaxed atmosphere and benefiting from it.

Infrequently, someone leaves a meeting not-too-happy about something which has been said. Even this is not all bad; it stimulates reflection, not on what was said, but on what was meant or what was accomplished at the meeting. And a better understanding ensues.

Due reflection on a program based on loving-kindness, a desire to learn and to understand and to help, deepens our appreciation of Al-Anon. It makes us work at meaning what we say and saying what we mean, and everybody gains.

All That's Needed

SOMETIMES SITUATIONS arise when I am helpless and I say, "All I can do is pray." That sounds apologetic and I am not, at all. I feel I am extremely fortunate that I can pray. For me, the Higher Power is God, my Father in Heaven.

I know there are others whom I consider less favored than I who do not so believe. In Al-Anon, however, they do have a Power greater than themselves which helps them through rough spots. None of us are alone anymore.

But I came on something recently in Pat O'Brien's WIND AT MY BACK, where he tells of a serious illness of their eldest child. His wife worked endlessly at her bedside and suddenly, miraculously, the child became better. His wife sought him and found him praying: "There was nothing else I could do," he told her.

"Nothing else was needed," she answered him.

There was my answer: I hope I never again say, "All I can do is pray." If there is something else to do, I'll do it and pray that I'm doing right. If things are out of my hands, I'll say, "I'll pray."

To me, prayer is a reaching, a stretching of myself, an earnest effort to become closer to God.

I feel that others who do not believe in God as I do have something which helps them—a member of a group I once belonged to felt her Higher Power was the group spirit and it never let her down; she practiced beautiful Al-Anon with this concept.

Because I write the FORUM some members think I know more Al-Anon than they do, that I have better answers. I wish that were true but I well know it is not.

Every one of us constantly learns from everyone else. Every one of us has some part of the program which means more to him than any other and which he understands better. But we all have a Higher Power on which we can surely rely.

Our 24-Hour Program

A WOMAN returned to our group after an absence of eight months. Something had happened which annoyed her and she heard herself making completely uninhibited charges which shocked her—but she kept on.

At the end of the scene she sort of came to and thought "I'd better get back to Al-Anon." Our meeting was on the Tenth Step, "Continued to take personal inventory and when we were wrong promptly admitted it."

This woman reminded me of myself in pre-Al-Anon days. I have visual proof and a powerful reminder of the Tenth Step: our china is Spode which we use for everything because of lack of cupboard space. The set came to me intact after my mother's death.

One night I got upset because things looked like the start of a binge and my husband came into the kitchen and harped on something which looked important in his confused state. A few minutes of this were enough to inflame me.

Ordinarily, self-control is my major pride; I can't abide loss of it in anyone, child or adult. That night I became so irritated I couldn't hang on to myself. I knew I should control myself but I didn't care. My eye lit on the dinner plates: I grabbed one, raised it high above my head and crashed it to the floor!

Even as I did it, watching myself in horror, I thought "This pattern is open stock. I can replace the plate." But

Mother had been dead ten years by then and it was no longer open stock, and I have never been able to get another.

Thus for all the years between, that plate I deliberately smashed and the scene I created always come to mind when I see the pile of plates. In the 20 years since then other plates have been broken and I've forgotten how. But I cannot forget that one—it's a constant reminder of how I once was and how much worse I'd be today without Al-Anon. Uncontrol, I believe, is also a progressive disease.

Thank God for Al-Anon; without it I might now have been tossing the whole set, and aiming not at the floor but at whoever or whatever was irritating me.

Al-Anon's is a twenty-four hour program. To many people this phrase means that we have only today in which to face our problems. It means that to me.

But it also means that we have to practice the program every minute of every twenty-four hours. We cannot swallow the program whole; we cannot leave it behind us in our meeting room. We have to take the Steps one at a time and make them our own, give them enough quiet thought so they are an integral part of ourselves—not something we take up and put down when we feel like "letting go."

Perhaps I am the only one in the world to whom a dinner plate "which isn't there" is a perpetual reminder of the Tenth Step. But it is certainly an effective one for me. Perhaps without Al-Anon and its self-discipline I'd never have been able to meet many difficult situations—for life itself presents constant problems. Al-Anon helps us meet them with courage and control.

The Person I'd Like to Be

SOMEWHERE in the glut of my indiscriminate reading, I picked up the idea that each man walks triply: the man he was, the man he is and the man he would like to be.

As all roads once led to Rome, after many years in Al-Anon, practically any new idea I meet quickly leads to consideration of it in terms of Al-Anon thinking. This concept of a triple-man appeared to me to be a *natural* Al-Anon idea.

Each of us knows the person he was, if we give it a little thought. If we are willing to be objective, each of us knows the person we are.

If we have been unhappy enough with the person we were, we have worked to change that person into one more suited to our ideals. We probably have not accomplished all the changes we desire, but we do get occasional glimpses of the person we'd like to be.

I do not know any Al-Anon member who was perfect to begin with, nor one who is perfect now. I do know numbers of them who have allowed anxiety, resentment and unhappiness to warp them, who have lost bright, sunny dispositions.

In this phase the person they were had become complicated by the person they are, and the unhappiness and discontent fortunately has driven them to Al-Anon, which, if they will work at it, will help them to become the person they would like to be.

For a guide to this end I can think of none better than the Prayer for the Day printed on the back of our little pamphlet "Just For Today" which sums it all up in the last lines:

"For it is in giving that we receive; it is in pardoning

that we are pardoned; and it is in dying that we are born to eternal life." To me, those are words to live by—ones I'd like never to forget as influences in making me the person I'd like to be.

The Wisdom of the Serpent

SERPENTS, to whom unusual wisdom is widely ascribed, have never been particularly appealing creatures. But I am indebted to one for a thought which comes to me often. He is G. B. Shaw's Serpent in "In The Beginning," who says to Eve, "You see things and you say 'Why?' But I dream things that never were; and I say, 'Why not?'"

Frequently I think of this at our weekly meetings when newcomers are present. Their burdens, their loneliness, their fears and resentments are so great that almost all they can say is "Why?" "Why did this happen to ME?" is implied if not said outright.

They know their own unhappy experience and find it difficult to believe that little or nothing of what they can tell is new or startling to the group. They do sense that the group has had help from something; there is an unmistakable atmosphere of acceptance and serenity which they feel and which usually makes them return to learn how to achieve it themselves.

More than half of our group are living with active problems, mates who have not yet accepted help or not even acknowledged they have a problem.

But Al-Anon's program has been of such help to the members that they can and do look forward to the day when things will straighten out. They can dream of this day which has not yet been and say to themselves, "Why not to us?" and they take heart.

It seems strange that all-too-often people find it easier to believe bad news than good. If they are unhappy, they dwell on that unhappiness, rather than look to a change.

So, to all those who see things and say "Why?" let Al-Anon show you how to dream things that never were and say to yourselves, "These things can come to me. Why not?"

Looking for God

". . . ONCE, from an interest in the history of mathematics, I was led into Blaise Pascal's *pensees;* he said that when you start looking for God, you have already found Him."

That, my friends, came not from inspirational reading but from one of my beloved mystery stories. Imagine! Gold *is* where you find it.

The above quotation contains a most moving thought. All too often, especially with newcomers to our program, one hears someone say, "I used to believe in God but through my difficulties I grew away from Him and no longer believed."

I do not think these people ever had lost God. They had mislaid their contact with Him for a time but He was there, waiting patiently, for Al-Anon to restore communication. Imagine the humility of God, waiting for *us.*

There are some people, however, who never had any belief to lose. But through Al-Anon, or some desperate experience previous to it, they, also, found God.

All through the Steps and Traditions there is constant mention of a Power Greater than ourselves, of our Higher Power and of God, even "God as we understand Him." Naturally this repetition starts something in their minds, when they see how it has served to help others. They, too, "come to believe."

Thus, for any who are still in that arid, unhappy desert where you feel yourself alone but sense there must be something else, remember: *there is.* Once you start looking for God, you have already found Him. He is there, simply waiting for you to call upon Him.

Remember also, we have been told, "Ask and ye shall receive. Knock and it shall be opened to you." Does it take much courage to ask? Since He has helped so many before you, is it difficult to believe that He will help you?

"Once you start looking for God, you have already found Him."

Ripening or Rotting?

As a child there were some of our family friends whom I instinctively avoided as much as I could. They were harsh, inflexible, and never laughed. Others drew me like magnets and I could spend endless hours with them, despite the gap in ages.

Later, as I grew up, I learned that tragic unhappiness had come to both sets. It used to bother me that one person had become so bitter and withdrawn that it was agony to be with him, while another, with equal cause, reached out a hand in friendship and welcome.

I was very fortunate in my parents, and in being one of eight children. No two people, with adult responsibilities, have time to spoil eight children. But they always had time to soften blows which come to all children, and to make us understand what was important and what wasn't.

Above all, they taught us we had a place in life and work

to do in it—that this was our work and no one could do it for us. We had responsibility as human beings, responsibility which increased as we grew older.

So I grew up, normally and happily, and was outgoing and seemingly well adjusted. But then came years of living with a problem too big for me, in ignorance, and alone.

The day came when I realized I was becoming one of the bitter, resentful people I'd avoided as a child. I had long since divided all adults into two classes; those who ripened and mellowed as they grew older, and those who simply rotted.

Unmistakably, I could see that I was rotting instead of ripening. But until Al-Anon showed me how to change I was helpless. I prayed for serenity, courage and wisdom. Gradually I improved. If I have not completely cured the rotting, I have at least arrested the tendency, and my everlasting thanks go to Al-Anon for what mellowing I have attained.

A Twenty-four Hour Program

DR. RUTH FOX has worked for many years with alcoholics. She has a deep understanding of them. I remember her telling of one patient who had had the greatest difficulty with the AA program. She listened and asked, "How long since you've been to a closed meeting?" He said he didn't care for closed meetings and never went, only to open ones.

"There's your trouble," she said. "Closed meetings are where you get the real AA program—where you get down to the brass tacks of it. Open meetings are the frosting on the cake."

Naturally I've never attended a closed AA meeting. I don't belong at one. But I'm sure I know what Dr. Fox meant.

Our Al-Anon speaker meetings are splendid and there's a lot to be learned by listening to other people's stories. But I believe there's more to be learned from a round-table discussion of the principles of the Al-Anon program.

When a speaker tells his story, it may or may not jibe with your own experience and thus may not be helpful. When you are having difficulty with any part of the program and ask for help on it, the whole group in a discussion meeting offers its best thinking on that one part alone and you are bound to be enlightened.

Those members who avoid meetings on the Steps or Traditions, and attend mostly the speaker meetings, I believe, show a lesser grasp of the program. They are attentive and listen well, it is true. But Al-Anon is a "sometime thing" with them, not a twenty-four-hour program. They are apt to leave the program behind them in the meeting room, not practice it in all their daily affairs.

It is only, I believe, when something happens which makes them put the whole program into practice, which makes them work at all phases of it, that they gain the very real help of Al-Anon.

When Evil Triumphs

SOMEWHAT SHORT of two hundred years ago Edmund Burke said, "All that is necessary for the triumph of evil is that good men do nothing." This comes to mind every time people write to say that their group is dying because one "Mrs. Al-Anon" will not give up . . . she feels it is her group and she must remain in authority.

To begin with, no one person in all Al-Anon has authority over a group or another Al-Anon member. "Our common welfare comes first." The First Tradition does not go on to say, "it comes first, last and always," but that's the way true Al-Anon works.

These correspondents with Mrs. Al-Anon-trouble always sound confused and very troubled. Naturally, it's a tremendously important problem and if they'd found the answer they wouldn't have written. But also they usually sound as if they'd done little to improve the situation—a bit as if they'd been Burke's good men who did nothing so that evil was flourishing.

What is there for them to do? First, I believe, an honest recognition of the situation calls for tremendous courage, a determination that the situation must be changed. In order to achieve this goal they must harden themselves to see it through, regardless of personalities, and not stop at the first setback.

I believe they can do nothing by talking among themselves and permitting it to continue. Rather, a few, two or three, should take the onerous and disagreeable task upon themselves of drawing up a blueprint of the group, pointing out what has happened to it—members dropping out, undercurrents, etc.—and privately presenting it to the overzealous chairman. I believe they should draw up By-Laws, group guides or whatever they want to call them, and see to it that they are not only adopted but followed. I believe that if the misguided chairman practices Al-Anon, she may temporarily be hurt and resentful but eventually she will see the light and will return.

But in this, as in many other situations, "all that is necessary for the triumph of evil is that good men do nothing."